FINDING HERSELF...
I WAS NOT HER!

PAMELA JAMES COLEMAN

S.H.E. PUBLISHING, LLC

For information contact: www.shepublishingllc.com

Cover and Title Page Design by Michelle Phillips of CHELLD3 3D VISUALIZATION AND DESIGN

ISBN: 978-1-953163-63-9

First Edition: February 2023

10 9 8 7 6 5 4 3 2 1

I would like to dedicate this book to

MARTHA JAMES
(1913-2023)

She protected me, cared for me
and loved me unconditionally

Thank you, granny.

CONTENTS

FINDING HERSELF...
I WAS NOT HER!

PAMELA JAMES COLEMAN

PREFACE

WHILE DRIVING HOME,
have you ever heard a song
That was so close to what you are going through
You had to pull over to cry?
That was me.

Anthony Hamilton's "Walk a mile in my shoes"

"Lost my wife, my cars, my home
I almost lost my mind, yeah
Oh, Lord
My Will was tested, got arrested
Was hard to keep me from crying
Oh, yeah"

This verse covers everything that happened to me since
moving out of my house.
There were so many times I didn't think
I would make it.

FLASHBACK

CHAPTER 1

HERE I STAND, IN THIS EMPTY HOUSE.

I look around thinking of the good times as well as the tough times. Not all times here were bad; we always had our annual family trip to South Carolina. That's why I love the beach so much. This started when Eric was six months old. We went every year until the year Kevin died. Christmas in this house was another favorite time of the year. It always looked like a department store once I was done with decorating the house.

The tears are starting to flow.

Wow. I haven't thought about this in years. I must sit down on the stairs. My head in hands, I think back to the times I thought about leaving, taking my two kids and just going. If I had thought I could take care of my boys, I would have left. I sat and wondered why I was staying. I looked at my paycheck. I thought, If I take the boys and start a new life, would that be the best thing for them? How would we survive?

I looked back over my life growing up. I thought that if my dad could do it, so could I. Kevin never laid a hand on me; he never raised his voice at me. The kids, on the other hand—it was on a regular basis.

I told him that when I heard a raised voice, it took me back to when my parents used to fight. I was uncomfortable with that. Every time I saw the boys cringe when he did it, I wanted to take them away from this. I wish I knew how I could take care of them. Like my father, I stayed.

I stopped cooking meals for the house, due to his questions about the way I would cook. His comments would be "I wouldn't have done it like that." My feelings were hurt. I didn't say anything because I didn't want to upset him. I didn't want anything about my home or marriage to look anything like my parents. My cooking wasn't the only thing he had comments on. My hair and clothes were also a subject of discussion. He loved long hair. One time I cut three inches off my hair. He went to my beautician and asked her not to cut my hair anymore. That didn't sit well with me. For years I thought it was a joke, but it wasn't.

The tears are really flowing now. When you hear the good outweighed the bad, it was a break even for me. He had been a true family-oriented person, but his parents and siblings came before we did. I saw so many traits of my mother that would come out. I remember that he took care of all the bills at the other house to the point that our electric would get turned off. We faced foreclosure on several occasions. I was not to tell his family because he had it under control.

When it was good, it was great. There was no middle of the road. Every time I thought about leaving, things became good. He did what he could to get to all the kids' events to show support. I continued to feel like a single parent. He worked twelve-hour days six days a week to keep both homes going.

Would this be the same as my mom and dad's marriage? I was scared to find out. As the years went on with me waffling back and forth to stay or to leave, we buried my grandmother, both his parents, and both my parents. Nothing could prepare us for what would happen between my dad's death and my mother's death.

I'm now standing looking back into an empty kitchen. The thoughts are flowing back as if it were yesterday. I had come home from work; it had been a good day in the workplace. I was shocked to see him home. He said he wanted to talk to me before the kids came home. I was leaning against the sink. He started with "I was hoping that I could manage this alone, but it's time for me to tell you. Months after your dad died, I was feeling bad. I went in for a checkup, and my PSA numbers were high. The doctors ran a test, and I have prostate cancer."

All I could think about was what he was going through, how we were going to tell the kids. I was numb. This wasn't the time to have any kind of breakdown. We sat at the table to go over his options and the game plan for telling the boys.

Any thoughts that I had or felt were now out the window. The focus was fighting this battle and winning. At that point, when he told me he had cancer, he was my husband of twenty-two years. He took care of our family—your parents, along with my family. I was now going to go to battle with you in this fight.

We began to take this fight head-on. Kevin was a person who didn't believe in taking or using medication, and we were about to start chemo treatment. His remedy to get rid of a cold was to wrap up in a sweat suit and a blanket, to make his body sweat out the cold or illnesses. I knew that this was going to be a fight in more ways than one way.

I need to sit back on the steps; the memories are coming back like a flood. Cancer is never easy. When you are asked not to tell anyone, it makes it harder than ever. I honored his request. I did tell my friend Elise about it, and she was at my house within two hours. I explained to her that I was not ready to have another loss in my life. She understood, and we talked for hours.

Every month his PSA numbers went up. We started out with oral chemo treatment, with no success. The doctors then moved to an aggressive chemo treatment; this slowed the progression down. While fighting this battle, my mother died in September, on my fiftieth birthday. His numbers started to stabilize. Only five people knew about this fight.

Until late December, his numbers were spiking. I tried not to worry because the doctors said that they had a new avenue of treatment. In January, we visited a specialist who had an experimental treatment. Once again, the numbers started to drop, and they stayed stable. We had gone through a lot. I had seen a side of him I had never seen. I was treated as an equal. I felt valued and needed.

We took the focus off his treatment and prepared for our last child to graduate high school. During this time of celebration, Kevin's numbers started to go up again. I told the doctors if they got to a point where they were going to give a timeline, would they call me first? They responded yes.

Evan's graduation was fun. The family was there. People were starting to notice that there was a change in Kevin, but I still didn't reveal his illness. It was time to plan our summer vacation. He looked so weak but insisted that we go. I wanted to take a dinner cruise, and he wanted to go fishing. I didn't like fishing, I thought that this could be the last trip that he would take to the beach like we had done every year since Eric was five months old.

Kevin's attitude began to change. He was short with us when talking. He became tired quickly. With that being said, I agreed to go on the fishing trip. It was a long trip from Virginia to South Carolina, and his ability to drive was getting bad. His sense of braking and awareness of other cars was very scary at times. I offered to drive, and he snapped with a reply that he had it, that I need not worry about it.

That wasn't the last time he snapped at me during the vacation. When we went out for breakfast, the service wasn't the best ever. On our way out the door, I stopped at the register to get the bill adjusted. Kevin and Evan went out to the car while I took care of that. It took a little bit of time to get help, Kevin returned to the restaurant, not the person that I had ever known before.

When he was lashing out at me and basically cutting me with his tongue, I walked to the car with tears in my eyes. I was trying to convince myself that it was the cancer that was changing his mood. When I sat down in the driver's seat, Evan knew something was wrong.

At that moment, I knew how my dad felt all the time when my mother would cut him with her words. At that very moment, I started to cry uncontrollably. When we pulled into the resort parking lot, Kevin looked over at me, and then he looked out the door with the remark "I don't have time for this. I have to go lie down."

I looked back at Evan, and I saw anger in his eyes. He came over to the car door and helped me out. He began with questions about what had happened in the restaurant. As I explained what had happened, he grew angry. I explained that the chemo treatment was making him act this way. Ignore it and enjoy the rest of your vacation.

It was September, my birthday month, and I had always looked forward to this month. I was the one who celebrated it the entire month. It was still a struggle with the month; it was almost a year ago when my mother died on my birthday. As I said before, she made sure she had the last say and that she would never be forgotten.

Monday morning while at work, I got a call that the time had come to give Kevin his timeline. I almost dropped the phone. I thanked them for letting me know. I would call his niece, who was just like his sister—I had promised her that if they ever were ready to give a timeline, I would let her know. She was devastated. I asked her if she could drive up Wednesday. They were going to tell him he had three months, possibly five, to live. She said she would be there without question.

Wednesday morning, Kevin began to have chest pains. I called the doctor; they requested that he come in earlier than his appointment. The doctors wanted to make sure he wasn't having a heart attack. I called his niece to let her know that they were going to tell him sooner rather than later. She made it in time for the appointment.

With five people gathered in the tiny exam room, he knew what was coming. I had heard the words over the phone, but there was something about hearing them in person, I had to step out of the room. The hospice called that night to set up a visit and to map out a plan going forward.

While I was on the phone with them, I asked if they could come over first thing in the morning.

Her response was yes, and she then asked me why so soon. I told her he was starting to transition. The nurse was shocked. She responded with "How do you know he is transitioning?" I told her that when she got here, she would see what I was talking about.

The next day, the hospice nurse arrived. As I had stated, he was starting to die. Kevin was no longer eating, drinking, or going to the restroom. It was now Thursday. The plans for three months took a quick and drastic turn. I called to update my friend Elise and just to talk. I couldn't understand how I could have another person die in September.

I stayed downstairs with Kevin. Thursday night we were unable to get him upstairs. He was starting to gain a solid weight. I looked up to the sky and asked my daddy to give me the strength he had to take care of mom.

Friday morning came, and the doorbell rang. It was Elise. I was so happy to see her. I don't think I could ever tell her how much her showing up meant to me. She stayed in the living room to talk to Kevin. Every time I would get out of his sight, he would call me. I would come over to where he was. His response was "OK, just checking." I know that went on another fifteen times.

The hospital bed arrived along with other medical items and a wheelchair. The nurse, Elise, and Eric took Kevin off the sofa and put him on the hospital bed. At this point I started to call the family. I wasn't sure if he would make it through the weekend.

His niece was completely shocked. She had just been there with us two days ago. They had said three months, not weeks. I called both of his doctors to let them know what was taking place. They were also in shock. They had just seen him two days ago, and there were no signs of him heading down this path.

His breathing was now labored, and relatives rushed to get there. He said that he needed to get to the lawyer's office on Monday. I didn't see that happening. As night started to fall, the hospice nurse stopped by the house. Kevin had now stopped all response.

As we stood in the room with him, the nurse, Elise, and I were talking about what the next few days might look like. I looked over at Kevin, and I knew we didn't have to talk about that anymore. He took a deep breath; he exhaled and was gone. Just like that—with one exhale, 24.5 years of my life were gone.

Now I am standing in the doorway of the room Kevin died in. I can remember it as if it were just last night. It's time to turn away and start anew. I don't want to reflect on the funeral and how I was treated. The sooner I stop with these flashbacks, the sooner I will be able to move—yes, move on.

2018 | THE MOVE

CHAPTER 2

WE BEGAN TO PACK UP 226 Blackthorn Lane the memories of packing this house up triggered more than could manage.

I remember how Kevin would say that my mom was a pack rat. I beg to differ; he was one. Our new home was smaller than 226, so I was not bringing that entire house to our new place. As we got Kevin's items together that we were not taking with us, I reached out to certain family members, to see if they wanted anything of his.

I told my boys as they were packing that if they hadn't touched something or worn it in a year, it wasn't going with us. As we slowly cleaned out the house, I had a dear family friend, George, come to work on the house so we could have it ready to sell. The work he was doing almost made me want to stay. I knew that this house would be more than I could possibly take care of. The maintenance alone would have taken a toll on me. I got a call from George; he said there was something in the master bathroom that he wanted to show me.

I went to the house after work to see what was going on. It was not good. When I got to the master bathroom, the wall behind the sink was gone. I didn't know what was happening, and when he began to explain, my heart sank. There was black mold covering the wall. I researched black mold. The internet said that black mold is extremely dangerous. Kevin was the only one who had used that bathroom for the last eight years. I stayed downstairs sleeping on the sofa.

Everything started to go through my mind. Was this the reason he got cancer? Did I need to get the boys checked? Did this travel through the air? Anything and everything was going through my head. I just sat on the floor, wondering about all the what-ifs. Then I realized that the what-ifs would do us no good now. Once I pulled myself together, I asked him to do whatever he needed to get it fixed and safe for resale.

Packing was completed, 226 had sold, the moving van was here, and it was time to make that move. As the movers started to take items out of the house, waves of emotions came over me. I was so scared. I was doing this alone, with no partner to help in this move. Evan was there, and he was amazing, but there would always be a void for a partner. I was worried—would I fail and let my kids down?

What would people say about me selling the home that I had shared with Kevin for over twenty-four years? Would they think that less than six months after he had died, I had sold the home and moved out? Would they think I was trying to ease or run from the memories of this house? Was this move the best thing for me and the boys?

I was wondering, was this move the right thing for us? I knew staying in this house would have a mixture of memories that would not be a good thing for any of us.

The process of building the new home was fun. I thought it would be stressful, but it wasn't.

We were now here; we had moved across the street from the home I had lived in for more than twenty-four years.

Our new home had all the personal touches done by Evan and me. I had to laugh because I had had two knee surgeries, and here I was in a home that had twenty-six steps to get to my bedroom.

I did this with the help of Evan to make it such a beautiful home. The kitchen counter was a rose color with gray in it that paired so nicely with the floor. We had gray hardwood floors throughout the house; the only rooms with carpet were the bedrooms. It was a dream for me to walk into my home with a smile.

Everything we did in this house was very personal, so when we came home, it was a welcoming feeling.

Evan got to design his living area. I think the most interesting part of our design was that he took the two bedrooms and had an archway put in the wall. Now he would not have to go out the door to get to the other room. It may seem like I was trying to run away from my past, but that is far from the truth.

While we were getting set up and settled into the new house, Granny made several trips to the hospital for shortness of breath. She decided that she wanted to stay in the nursing home.

If I didn't sell her home, we would be unable to get her into the nursing home of her choice. I reached out to the APS (Adult Protective Services). When they did an in-home visit, they would be able to move things along to get her into the nursing home if they didn't feel she was safe living alone. I explained to Granny that she would need to let them know that she would need help as long as she was in her home.

She ran off the people that I had coming in twice a week, saying she didn't need them. After an hour of them talking to my grandmother and asking her questions, she would reply that she was fine and didn't need any help. With a survey of the home, they knew that she needed help.

We talked for a while in the driveway. I wasn't prepared for what she was going to say next. It could be thirty to sixty days before they would be able to get her out of the home. The positive was that she was going to the help that was needed.

Not a full week later, she called me to let me know she was having breathing problems. She had a breathing treatment machine like they use in the ER. Unfortunately, I didn't know how to use it. I called my sis-friend Shanti to help me.

Granny was fifteen minutes from my house, and Shanti was thirty minutes from me. But Shanti got in her car late at night to drive forty-five minutes to help me and my grandmother. Once we got the treatment going for her and she seemed to show some signs of improvement, I told her I was going to stay with her, and she refused. We both left; she seemed better.

Early the next day, my phone rang, it was the rescue squad calling from her house. They wanted to let me know that they were taking my grandmother to the hospital, and she wanted me to meet her there. I got dressed and gave them the fifteen minutes it would have taken me to drive. I was good at my guessing—she was there, and she looked so pitiful.

I called the family members to let them know where she was. I also called APS to let them know that she was in the hospital. I saw this as my opportunity to round up the troops to help clean her house. If she came home, the kitchen, bathroom, and bedroom would be the clean that I would love to see.

I took off two days from work to clean her house and to be there for anything the doctors might need. I was called in for a meeting with the doctors and APS. It was somewhat good news—they both agreed that she needed to be in a facility; it would be the safest thing for her. She would get around-the-clock care; she would have people to talk to all day if she wanted to.

I was preparing myself to tell her the news, not sure how she was going to take it. The doctor went in with me. He explained to her what he thought would be the best thing for her. You would have thought it was Christmas, how excited she was. What pulled at my heartstrings was that she was worried about me being worried about her. She told the doctors that she didn't want to put added pressure on me, trying to work, take care of the boys, and go places.

It was nothing new for us to worry about each other. I wiped the tears from my eyes and started working with APS to get her to the nursing home. The transaction went smoothly, and she was all set and ready to go. I remembered my dealings with Medicaid and my mother. I contacted my realtor ASAP.

I thought this was going to be a tough sale, due to the state that the house was in. It wasn't on the market for a week; we had a full offer from the owner of the farm across from the house. He wanted to buy it for his stable hands to live in during the week.

This was a win for both of us. I sold the house to take care of my grandmother, and it would stay in the hands of someone we somewhat knew. If you thought that was the hard part, think again. I got a dumpster delivered to the house.

I had a five-person crew collaborating with me. Several days prior to the help coming, I went through the house and put Post-it Notes on the things that needed to go. My brother had to find a way to get his items out of the house. We were making prompt progress until the dumpster was full, and we hadn't put a dent in the house at all.

Shanti's husband started putting as much in his van as he could until the other dumpster got there. In the meantime, we started a chute or slide out the second-floor window to get the items from upstairs. My grandmother always said that if anything happened to her, it would take an army to clean her house out because she had all her grandmother's items, her mother's items, and her brother's items, plus her own. That was an understatement. We found sheets that would crumble apart when you picked them up. That was how old things were in that house.

I told my brother that I would help him out with his items, since he had a load of stuff. I told him that I would pay for a storage unit for him for a year to give him time to find a place for it or whatever his plans were for them. I refused to go through what I had gone through when I sold Dad's house.

He would not have the opportunity to put in the streets that I had sold Dad's house, taking his inheritance, I find that hard to believe, when I had given him both of daddy's cars, and everything in the house. When Daddy's house was sold, I took out my Diana Ross doll, two year-books, and my wedding veil.

I wasn't in the mood to go through that again with him. The last time had been more than I wanted to deal with. I reminded him of what Granny wanted him to have. She wanted the boys to have a chair from the house. I didn't really understand why she wanted them to get a chair, but it hit me. The chairs that she was talking about were the chairs that they sat in when they were smaller.

I took out of the house the items that meant the most to me. I got a magazine rack, my dad's highchair, and a chest. For me, if there's nowhere to put it in my house, then there is not a need to take it with me.

The house was now clean. I sat there for a little bit to take in everything. This was the place I would go to when I needed to feel safe. This was the house that my father would take me to as a haven from all that was going on in my house. This house had been all I had known since I was little, and now it sat empty and was going into someone else's hands.

I stood in the doorway one last time. All the dinners and Christmas and Thanksgiving gatherings were now over. Everything this house had meant to me was now treasured memories. As I closed the door for the last time, it was like closing a chapter of my life.

On my ride home, I had so many thoughts going through my head. I hoped that this would be the last door that I would have to close to an empty house, that this was the last door that I would close to memories. I hoped this would be the start of my life of happiness.

Granny's room was nice. It was a single room with her own bathroom. She also had a patio. This made me feel better—that she had a semblance of home. She made friends fast. She was exercising by going to bingo and doing crafts. Her spirits seemed to get better. What a turnaround for her. The staff was calling her Granny, so I knew then she was well cared for and that I had nothing to worry about.

The nursing home had events for the residents. Church was her favorite; I was glad it was there. One of the things I remember growing up was her in the kitchen making multiple dozens of dinner rolls for the church on Sundays. Her friends came to see her. I couldn't ask for better arrangements for her.

I had a close friend who was a travel agent. She knew that I had been wanting to go back on a cruise for a while, and she found a great package leaving out of Maryland. We made it a mother-son trip—she brought her son, and I brought mine.

We had an amazing time. I think the food was Evan's favorite part of the trip. For me it was to get to spend time with him, to see the look on his face—being on a cruise was special for me. I was able to do something for him that he had never done before.

I am not sure how much he will remember of the trip; I know this is one that will stay close in my heart for a long time to come. I was able to check in on Granny while we were gone, which was a big bonus for me. I had never played bingo a day in my life—we were on vacation; why not?

I really did upset the regular bingo players. The first time out, I won three games. Evan was telling me about the stares I was getting. Man, I didn't care. We were winning money to spend, and it didn't have to come out of pocket. I became a bingo junkie, and by the end of the trip, I was able

to pay the entire tab we had with our winnings only. To me

that was a win. Evan, on the other hand—I gave him forty

dollars to gamble with my friend's son. He went to the

blackjack table and lost twenty dollars. He put the other

twenty in his pocket and didn't gamble for the rest of the trip.

He would stand behind me or sit in the seat next to

me while I played the slots. I was winning there also. I can't

begin to tell you how much fun I was having. I got thirty

dollars in scratch tickets. I won five dollars, which got my

bingo cards for the night.

You could put your nonwinning tickets in this large

tub. On the last day of the cruise, they would pull out tickets

to spin the wheel for more prizes. I was playing the slots.

They called my name, and someone yelled, "It's the bingo

lady!" I couldn't control my laughter. I won another fifty

dollars in scratch tickets, and from that I got thirty. I split it with Evan. He sat next to me and played. He won his twenty dollars back and stopped.

This was an amazing trip. Now it was back to work and taking care of my grandmother. I came home for the day to get a punch in the stomach. It was a good one, yet a sad one. I didn't know that Evan had applied for college. He was ready to go back and try it. My heart was breaking into a million pieces, as his mother, I was going to support him.

He was so excited; he had gotten into a school in West Virginia. I was happy for him yet sad for me because it felt like I was losing another family member. But we had the summer, so I wasn't going to worry too much. We had trips to take and just have fun. We had gone through so much that it was time to finally enjoy life.

For those who don't know, our family is into racing of all types. Evan is an F1 fan, and he found an F1 race that was close to us. This race was going to be in Texas in

October. I told him to check the dates because his aunt was getting married, and I didn't know what weekend it was. Wouldn't you know—the weekend he wanted to go to Texas was the same weekend as the race.

I suggested he look at other races, and we would see what we could do. During the summer there was a race in Canada. I told him he could get with our friend, have her set it up, and let's go. While that was being planned, my best friend Elise was planning her fiftieth birthday party.

She was taking her close friends and family to Jamacia for the week. I had to take Evan to school, and the dates sounded the same. That also worked out. I had to have him at school on a Wednesday, and everyone was leaving on Friday, so that worked out great.

Our Canada trip was here. I, along with Evan, was getting so excited. He had made a list of food items we had to try while we were there. Once we arrived at the hotel, which was nice and near everything, Evan had out his food list. He started to map out the restaurant compared to where we were staying.

We decided not to move the car unless we really had to. This was not a problem—everything we needed was within walking distance. We walked to what seemed like a downtown area. They had vendors out and live music; it was so inviting. The people were super friendly. We continued our stroll around Montreal. During this outing we found a mall. It looked like an apartment building until we saw the shoe store name on the outside. When we went in, it was like an apartment building with the center missing.

This place was seven stories high. While we were in there looking around, we both forgot that there was a price exchange, so what we thought was expensive was really in our price range. What a lesson we had in trying to do the exchange to know what we were going to be charged.

On the walk back to the hotel, I told him that I was hungry. I knew we were going to get something we hadn't had before. We stopped at Subway—yes, we got subs and took them back to the hotel. I told him we didn't go over one thousand miles to eat the Virginia way. Why did this child fall into the wall laughing at me?

Next on the food side of things, I asked him, "What is the plan for food today?"

"We must try poutine."

I asked, "What are you having us eat?"

He started to laugh and said, "It's French fries with gravy and cheese."

I gave him a blank stare. I didn't understand—gravy is for mashed potatoes only.

"If you think about it," he said, "french fries are spuds. Not any difference." He had a point.

I said, "Let's go, friend."

We had so much fun cutting up on the stroll. We got to the restaurant; it was a house turned into a restaurant. We sat outside to take in this new food item. I must say it was a sizable number of fries, and I will leave the rest alone. Not to offend those who live there, but it's an acquired taste.

Now it was time to go to the race. This was the main reason for our trip—what an experience. Seeing the smile on Evan's face was priceless. He was in his element. There were things I didn't understand about this race, and he didn't mind explaining them to me.

For one, why were the people of Montreal booing his driver? It was partly the driver but more so the manufacturer. The race went fast, and we had enough time to look around before we left. When we got back to the hotel, there was an F1 shop close by. We walked there so he could stock up on racing gear.

While we walked over, I was snapping photos like crazy. I told Evan that I wanted to do something different on every trip we took. I began to look for things to do. The one we landed on was going to the top of the tallest building in Montreal. It was also a tourist stop.

I still to this day don't understand why someone who is afraid of heights always wants to do things that involve heights. On one trip to South Carolina, my husband and I jumped out of an airplane. Now this. When I reached the top of the building, I was scared. Like every tourist, you want your photo op. I walked slowly to get as close to the window as my heart would allow. I took photos, then walked extremely fast back to the center to enjoy the rest of what the top floor had to offer.

It was kind of funny because you must take different elevators to get to the top. For whatever reason, that made me feel better. Something about if the cable to the elevator broke, it wasn't the full thirty-plus floors to drop. I know that sounds funny, but I felt better about it.

Once Evan was through entertaining me, it was time to go back to the mall. I saw shoes that I wanted, and so did Evan. We both knew that we would get shoes that no one at home would have. I said we must eat somewhere else on his food list. He had a pizza place on his list. We had a good dinner and went back to the hotel to pack. Time to return home and prepare to take my son to school in a few weeks.

I don't think we had been home two hours when my phone rang. The nursing home was calling to let me know they were taking my grandmother to the hospital for breathing issues. I was back on the clock, and I hadn't been home for two hours. When I got there, she was doing well; this was the first time the nursing home had seen one of her breathing attacks. The ER gave her a breathing treatment, and she was fine. Back to the nursing home within four hours.

Summer was ending. As we got closer to Evan leaving, I would get sad. I tried to focus my energy on the fact that not two days after dropping him off at school, I would be heading to Jamacia with my sis-friends.

I planned a little going-away party for him, and we had an enjoyable time. The people who meant the most came to his going-away party. As you grow up, you realize that quantity over quality is more important. I did well during the party—no tears; there was so much laughter in the room, we didn't have time for tears.

The day was here, one that I was so proud of and sad about, all at the same time. I would be in the house alone; there would be no one there if something happened to me. WAIT, WAIT...this was something that my mother would say. I was nothing like her, and I would not let that come to the surface.

Evan started to wake up. I looked in the mirror; my eyes gave away that I had cried the entire night.

I looked at Evan. I told him, "Let's do this. It's time for you to go with your friends, play football, and enjoy your life." On the four-hour drive, we laughed and talked about our Montreal trip and what he should do if there was an emergency, since I was four and a half hours away from him. Our plan was in place.

The closer we got to the school, the more I was looking around taking in the surroundings. I looked at him. I asked, "Where are we, son?"

Evan let out one of the largest laughs. His response was "Deep country, Mom. Deep country."

I looked back at him with such a serious look on my face and responded, "No shit."

We laughed for a good ten more miles.

We got to the school in time to get ourselves together. We found his dorm. I was mentally prepared to set his room up, which he would share with a roommate. I was so very wrong; he had his room to himself. The only thing he had to share was the bathroom. We got all his stuff out of the car and into his room. I was getting ready to set his room up, and a hand landed gently on my arm. "I got it," Evan said.

I am not sure why that hit me so hard. This was the last thing I could do before I walked away, not to see him for a while. It was not the time to be selfish. I stopped. "No problem, friend. Let's go get the other stuff done, and I will hit the road. I need to pack."

So we had parent orientation in the gym, and I was sitting there crying like I was experiencing a death. I looked to my right, and there was another mom going through the same pain. We smiled at each other; something about seeing each other with the same struggle made this better.

The parents went outside to meet up with the kids. My biggest challenge with this day so far was to get my face fixed and fix it with urgency. I saw him walking toward me. I put on a fake smile and laughed. Evan was very funny. His response was "So you been crying again."

I really burst out laughing at that point. He knew me too well.

I told him to get in the car. "Let's go to the general store to get the stuff you are missing and extra food."

The store was really like a general store from back in the day. It worked for the students there—it had food, household items, like paper plates, laundry detergent. Things they could purchase until their parents could come visit.

It was time to leave. I made sure he had everything he needed. I wanted to hug him, but I knew what would happen. I got smart. I asked him, "You want a hug?"

He laughed hard. "A knuckle bump would be fine."

A knuckle bump it was. Then I grabbed him and gave him a big hug. I turned quickly and started walking. With a quick turn and a wave, I started to walk toward the car. The tears started to flow vigorously. By the time I got to the car, I was crying so hard that I was starting to throw up.

I got into the car. On my way home, the phone rang. It was Evan. He had forgotten something in the car. Oh no! I must go back. I had to do this again. My heart couldn't take it, but for him I would do anything. I made a quick U-turn. Thank goodness what he needed was in the back of the car, and I didn't have to get out.

He popped the trunk to grab what he needed and told me to hurry home before it got dark. "OK, friend, I will let you know when I get home." I don't know how I made it to the highway. I cried and cried for a good forty-five minutes. I put on my driving tunes; I was now homeward bound.

Four and a half hours later, I was home. I sent a text message to let Evan know that I was home. He was out with his friends and new bathroom mate. That made my heart feel good. I could go on this trip knowing that he was OK and getting adjusted. School would not be a problem.

I sat down on the sofa with a glass of wine. The house was so incredibly quiet. I wondered how I was going to get used to it. What I was feeling was selfish—this was not about how I was going to make it. It was about my son growing into his own.

I had almost finished the entire bottle when my phone rang. It was my sister's friend wanting to know if I was ready to go.

This deserved a laugh. "Hell no, I am not ready. Give me a little bit, and I will be ready."

That call got me pumped up to leave. With the music now blasting throughout the house, I was packing and looking forward to being in Jamacia within the next forty-eight hours.

I stopped by the nursing home to see Granny. I wanted to make sure that she had all her snacks and clean clothes for the week I would be gone and to let the nurses know whom to contact in my absence if there was an emergency.

Everyone was taken care of. Now it was time for me to have fun.

We made it to Jamacia without any issues. It was such a beautiful place. It was my second time there, and I can say that it was still, if not more breathtaking if not more so than the last time I was there. My friend had our arrangements beyond perfect. I shared a suite with her and her friend from Alabama. It was nice to meet new people and have an enjoyable time.

When my sister-friend wasn't around, we started to plan a surprise dinner on the beach for her. The hotel made it so special; everything was amazing. The surprise was almost ruined by the hotel. We had everything set up. The staff put the bill under the door. The statement had her name on it, and she was getting upset that there was this crazy charge on her bill.

It took convincing that she didn't need to go downstairs to figure out what was wrong. We told her to trust us—all would be OK. She thought that we were dining at one of the restaurants at the resort. She was concerned when we took a turn outside and it was dark. "Where are we going?" she asked.

We kept walking. No one was saying a word.

Once we got to the edge of the sand, it was breathtaking. There was a large round table to seat six, covered in white linen. Everything was white except for the beautiful centerpiece. She was shocked as well happy that we had taken the time to plan this for her.

The meal was amazing. We ate under the light provided by a spotlight and bamboo lights. There was laughter as well as tears as we all took turns telling Elise what she meant to us. As our dinner concluded, we thought it would be interesting to see what the in-house nightclub was all about.

Momma H walked up but thought she would return to the room to prepare for our excursion the next day. As we approached the door, the door the music was loud. You would have thought that this place was packed. Just the opposite. We walked in, and there was the DJ, two drunk people dancing, and one man sitting alone.

The total number of people at this club, if that's what you want to call it, was four people. And then you added us, and it was a total of eight. The drinks were free, so we all went to the bar and started to drink. This made the music better, and no one cared that no one was in the room. We all just danced with ourselves. We were having a fun time, and then the man who was sitting alone made his way over to Elise.

This was something we were all used to. We would always give her a tough time that we couldn't take her anywhere with us if we were trying to meet someone because they would go straight to her. He seemed like a nice person, so I didn't comment on Elise talking to him. When the music started to get weird, we all left, and the guy walked out with Elise. I wasn't ready to go to sleep like the others. I sat outside on the deck and listened to the waves, thinking about Evan and wondering if he was doing OK.

I was asleep in minutes; it was so relaxing. When I got up to go inside, Elise was sleeping on the lounge chair next to me. This place was so beautiful. I had to go to bed to get ready for our excursion tomorrow. We were going on a party boat during the day. It was going to be fun.

We arrived at the dock, or secluded beach area. As soon as we got there, we were greeted with a drink of choice and lunch. I believe it was to coat our stomachs for all the alcohol we were about to consume on the boat. It was time to board. There were people getting on the boat.

The first thought that rolled through my mind was, I can't swim. If this boat tips over because we have too many people, someone is going to have to save my ass. With drink in hand and beach bag in the other hand, I got on the boat. We were traveling over to Dunn's River. Dunn's River is one of Jamacia's special places, two miles of waterfalls that you can climb. I said to myself, this should be safe, right?

On the way over we couldn't drink any alcohol due to being around the water.

When we got to the waterfall, it was amazing. I was having second thoughts about going up it, but I didn't want to miss this opportunity again like I did on my honeymoon. So, I put on my big-girl pants and joined the rest of them.

Going up this waterfall, we had to go in a chain-like line so that if someone slipped, the chain would hold on to them. Sounds safe; OK, let's go. So why, not halfway in, did I slip? There was no harm done, so we kept going. There was someone taking photos, so you wouldn't have to worry about making sure you got photos.

Now we were traveling through this cave-like structure. Elise's sister slipped, and her leg went down into a crack. She was bleeding a little, but you could tell that this was going to hurt later. While we were helping her up, guess who fell in the same location. Yes, I slipped into the same hole that sissy did. The difference was I got wedged between the rocks and needed help to get out. Once out, I could tell that my leg and thigh were bruised. The tour guide said that we could stop at the first landing and walk back to the boat.

We both refused to stop. As we continued to climb the waterfall, I could see why this was the main attraction. I can't begin to describe the beauty that was there. It was a calm, peaceful feeling. I couldn't tell that there were fifty people around me.

As we continued, there was a lagoon that we had to cross. I can't swim, so it was rather a challenge. I was not going to let my family down. I hopped on the slide, and off I went into the water. I played it off, but I was scared.

We finally reached the top, and looking back to see what we had done, I had a feeling of accomplishment.

Now back to the party boat. Remember I told you Elise could pull all the men? There was this attractive crew member on the boat that we all were drooling over. He looked down, saw our group, and went straight to her. We all started to laugh because we knew it would happen. She was beautiful. The music started playing, and we had a great ride back. Well, that is until we hit dry land. Sissy and I had had all the free drinks we could manage. It was a rum punch, and when we started to walk or tried to walk, it was nothing short of hilarious.

Our beautiful vacation was ending, and my mind was going back home. I would return to an empty house, and the tears started to flow. I knew that I would see Evan in a few weeks. For the first time, I was truly alone. We returned to Virginia with no issues. Our other party guests returned to Alabama safely as well.

I was home, and the house was empty—no noise, no one playing video games. I went to my room, unpacked, and started to wash clothes. I found myself in Evan's room on his bed in tears. I pulled myself together, and I thought, why not call Evan, just to see how he's doing?

I'm glad I did. He told me how football practice was going. The statement that had been made to him was not what was happening. He was being used as a practice dummy. Not really working out with the team, as he was told. I asked him what he wanted to do. He was not there on a scholarship; we were paying the bill. His response was "Let me think about it."

He went on to tell me about his bathroom mates and the food in the café. I think the funniest thing for me was the story of five people getting in the car to drive thirty-five minutes to get to Walmart. Then he asked when I was coming up there to get him. I couldn't do anything but laugh.

I responded that I would be there Friday evening when I got off from work. It was Labor Day weekend. I was looking forward to seeing him. I left work two hours early, which was good. I was able to get to West Virginia in the daytime. The roads to get to the school were super winding, and my night-vision driving is not the best. Let's not add rain into the equation, and oncoming traffic. I am no good at driving.

We made it back home safely. Evan came home with his dirty laundry, of course, and a lengthy list of needed items along with food. I really think it was cheaper to keep him at home. I didn't know how fast a weekend could go. We were back on the road. This time when I dropped him off, the tears were less. I guess knowing that he was OK helped with my tears.

I was home. I found myself getting used to having the house to myself. I didn't have to peep out the door to run downstairs for coffee with little or no clothes on. I could walk downstairs with pride. I played the music I wanted to hear, watched the shows I wanted to watch. I was really getting used to this.

Thanksgiving was here. I made my trip over the mountain and through the wood. Yes, it felt like it. This trip was different; it wasn't Evan and me on this trip. We had his bathroom mate with us. Sam was such a nice young man; I now had another adopted son. I told Evan that it was OK if he stayed with us for Thanksgiving if he wanted to.

Evan said that his parents were coming to pick him up from our house. They lived an hour away; it was easier for me to pick him up since we were heading in the same direction. Sam and Evan had become good friends fast. That eased the worry that I had. I knew that he had his high school friends there; sometimes it's good to have your own crew.

What I thought would never happen did. I had gotten used to the house being empty, and now I heard laughter and yelling at the computer screen. I had to shut my bedroom door. It was still nice to have him home, but I had gotten used to the fact that we were going to do this for the next four years. Or would we?

It was Thanksgiving Day. I looked at the sign over the stove: "The queen don't cook." The queen was me. The queen had dinner delivered to the house. All I had to do was throw baking flour on my face, and no one would have known. Dinner was a little quiet and awkward—not sure why—then Evan, just matter of fact like, said, "I am not going back next year."

I can't begin to tell you about the look on my face when he said that. Part joy that he was coming home and the four-hour-plus drive we didn't have to take. The other look that I had was WHAT! I had just gotten used to you being gone, and now I must get used to you coming back. Oh, Lord.

I began with a host of questions. "Why do you want to leave? What's going on? How in the hell did we get here when you just said a month ago you were doing great?"

His response was "This is not a fit for me, I don't want to stay and waste money when I know that, at the end of the day, this is not working."

I sat there for a little bit, eating my dinner and thinking about what he had said. I reflected on Eric's struggles getting through school. Always wondering what we could have done differently. I slowly stopped eating. My response was simple: "Is this what you really want to do?"

He replied, "Yes. I am ready to come home and join the workforce."

With that being said, I agreed with his decision, but under one condition. He was to stay at the school until the end of the semester. I wanted him to have one semester of college under his belt. When he filled out applications, he would be able to check the box for college. They never asked you how much; it just said "some." That box would help his application move up the chain of review a bit faster.

On the drive back from West Virginia, I started to process the things I wanted to get done in the next thirty days. I was feeling thankful that Evan was able to notice that college was not for him. The big question was, what was he going to do for work? Would he take classes online? What would he do? I said to myself that I would let that be in the back of my mind for a little while. I would cross that bridge when I got to it.

I had an idea: Evan had been researching a miniature Siberian husky. When I got back to work, I started looking for one for him for Christmas since he would be home to work with him. Doing a serious internet search, I found the cutest little puppy. I was thinking, Would the puppy be better with us if he came with a sibling? The lady I was working with thought it would be a clever idea for them to travel together. She had experience with customers getting two puppies and having no problem. After talking to her, I was on board getting two. I wanted this to be a surprise for Evan. He was getting this for a Christmas gift. It would be one he would know about before Christmas arrived.

I was going to call Evan to tell him what I had done. I changed my mind. I thought this would be a pleasant surprise for him when he got home. Three weeks seemed to go by extremely fast. It was time for me to pick up Evan from school.

My four-hour drive seemed to go by fast. There they were, Evan and Sam waiting like two little kids at the day care, knowing it was time for their parents to pick them up. I had to do a double take of all the stuff Evan had to bring back home. I didn't remember bringing up that much stuff.

Then it hit me—when he returned from Memorial Day weekend, he took another carful.

I looked at both of them and shook my head. I asked, "Where are we going to put all this mess?" They started laughing like I had told a joke. I opened the hatch, sat on the sidewalk, and watched them make it work. To this very day, I have no clue how they managed to get all those items into the car.

On the return home, Evan asked if it was OK if Sam stayed with us for a few days, until his parents could pick him up. I didn't have any problem with that. Sam was a good young man. He never gave me any reason to think something would happen while I wasn't there.

When we got home, I had held on to this secret long enough. Evan came downstairs, and I said to him, "Guess what?"

As always, he gave me that look like "go ahead."

I told him that we were going to pick up one of his Christmas gifts.

He perked up then. "What is it?"

"I got you the doggie you wanted."

The smile on his face made all that I had gone through and the amount that that little puppy cost worth it.

We were now dog owners again, and this time it was twice the fun. We noticed that the two puppies were not getting along. We did research and learned that two male puppies have problems being raised together. I was a bit upset because the lady who sold him to me could have told me of that. During December, we did everything we could to keep the two pups together.

We had the dogs in separate crates during the night. The only time that they were together, they were running through the house playing. It was when the rough playing began and we were unable to tell whether it was play or serious that they needed to be broken up.

2019 | WHERE'S THE MONEY

CHAPTER 3

CHRISTMAS BREAK WAS ENDING, and we had to make tough choices. Would we continue to break up the puppy fights? Would we rehome one? If we rehomed, I knew which puppy it would be. I had gotten the puppies for Evan as a Christmas gift, so I wouldn't take his puppy away from him. This was such a hard decision to make.

After talking with Evan, I said, "We can give the pups until the end of January to see how they work out." I was hoping that they would grow into being with each other, to keep each other company. That didn't happen. Now it was time to make a hard decision.

We rehomed the one that was mine. His name was Caine, short for the drink hurricane, which I had had in New Orleans. The manager at a local pet store gave him a home. I knew that he would be well cared for. She always wanted a pup like Caine, but she couldn't afford one. She knew him well from coming into the store, getting treats and toys. I felt good about him going home with her. I was a little sad, but it had to be done for everyone's safety.

Now our focus was on Trunks, the remaining puppy, to get him trained. The training went very well except the potty-training part. I would take him outside, and this dog would play outside the entire time. As soon as we stepped foot into the house, he would do his business.

After a month of this fight, I found in-home puppy training. Trunks would be there for two weeks. Evan and I were excited about this; we both knew that he would come back trained. Trunks's training was at the perfect time. I wanted to share with Evan how much fun Jamacia was, and with Trunks at the trainer, we could slip away one time without getting a sitter. A week later, I got a phone call that he wanted to keep Trunks for another week at no charge. I couldn't believe it; this dog was failing puppy camp. I knew this must be a first.

Evan and I went to Jamacia for spring break. It was fun to have my travel friend with me. On this trip, the winds were blowing at fifteen to twenty miles per hour. It was easy to get sunburned; you couldn't tell that you were getting hot because of the breeze. In the hotel that we were in, the elevator was out of order, along with the air conditioning. This was not the impression I wanted Evan to get. The nonstop food he could eat all day was the part that he liked the most.

We went to a silent dance party. We watched a dance competition and a water volleyball game. Even if we didn't do as much as the last trip, I got him out of the hotel room, and I saw a few smiles, which made me smile.

It was time to return home. I was hoping that we were going back to good news about Trunks.

We met the trainer to pick Trunks up, and he was so happy to see us. The trainer shook his head. He didn't understand why this puppy wouldn't train to go to the bathroom. He apologized and wished me luck, then he drove off. I didn't even get to ask what suggestion he had for us.

In the weeks to come, this little dog wreaked havoc throughout the house. I was going to the laundromat wash the puppy pads. We were still going through the I-don't-want-to-potty outside, even when we would stay outside with him for over an hour to make sure he would go. Every time, he would come back in, go to his crate, and potty.

We were now back to the drawing board. I didn't want to seem like a failure to the little guy. I had to do something. Our home was now smelling like a barn or a puppy kennel. I asked Elise's sister if she knew anyone who would love to take care of the little fellow and help him find a forever home.

She started to work on it for us. Elise's sister called me back. She said that she would take him in until he could get home. We drove Trunks about thirty miles to his temporary home. He seemed to fit in with the other puppies she had.

I thanked her for her help. As I was walking away, I just started to cry. At that moment I decided that I would no longer try to be a dog owner, living in a house with no grass.

With all that went on with the training, the holidays were good. Evan was happy with the puppy; we just wished it had turned out differently.

As we drove off, Evan and I both agreed that we were not going to do the doggie thing again. I asked him if he would like to go anywhere for the summer. His answer was no; he was good.

I was OK with that; I would have time to spend with Granny over the summer. I had big plans for the house. I know that we had all the pictures up and the furniture was in place, but there were the trivial things that I wanted to do.

I had my dad's highchair and two little chairs I sat in when I was in day care that I wanted to refurbish. To have a summer when I didn't go anywhere was so exciting to me.

The last two months of school went by like a blur. Evan met me at the door to tell me he had an idea for his room. I was nervous about what he was going to say, and I was right.

He wanted to paint his room orange. I felt the color leave my body. I smiled and responded, "Sure." Now I was not looking forward to summer. I laughed to myself. It was his room; if he wanted to try orange, have at it.

School was over, time for projects. Evan did change his mind about the orange; his room stayed the same color. I got patio furniture delivered. I just knew that I was going to spend time out on the deck reading a book, sipping wine the entire summer.

I was wrong. July came, and Elise and I ended up in Cincinnati, Ohio. I had never been to Ohio, so why not go? Ohio was having a music festival with fifteen different artists performing. I had such a fun time. This was my first trip that I had taken without going to Granny's to make sure she was

OK. I asked my sister-in-law to check in on her for me. I think the only time I was in the hotel room was to sleep; that's how much fun we were having. This year was going by so fast, I had only a couple of weeks left before school started. It felt like we had only been out of school for two weeks, which was how fast it went by. Evan was hired to work at the high school. I didn't have to worry about him. If he had money, would he get a job that he liked? All those thoughts were now put to rest.

It was August, and I was preparing for the start of school. The phone rang. It was the nursing home saying that they were sending my grandmother to the hospital. I left work to meet her in the emergency room. As I was driving there, I knew that it would be the same thing, that she was having a tough time breathing and once she got a treatment, all would be OK.

Upon my arrival at the emergency room, I walked into my grandmother's room. She was very pale, couldn't breathe, and was having a tough time talking. I sat with her for a while waiting for the doctors. Her family doctor came in. He wanted to run tests, but he felt like her heart was shutting down, and things didn't look good.

When they took her off for testing, I called the family to let them know what the doctor said, and when I got more information, I would let them know. When she returned from testing, her doctor said that they would like to keep her in the hospital. Once she got a room, we would talk more.

Now the feeling that I had had that this was normal was no longer. What was going on? What were they going to tell me? Was I ready to lose another loved one? I should be at peace with this if it was her time to go; she was over a hundred years old. She had always said that she had seen it all and done it all. If she could have given Kevin twenty years of her life so he could have stayed here, she would have.

We were settled in her room, she was comfortable and talking a little bit, and she seemed to understand what was going on. She grabbed my hand to tell me everything was going to be OK. Then she drifted off to sleep.

In came the doctors. None of them showed signs of a positive statement coming. They began. "Your grandmother is a remarkable lady to have seen the number of years that she has. Going over her test results, we don't feel she has much time left with us."

My heart sank. It was only a matter of time; her little heart couldn't continue to manage moving the excess fluids around. I took a deep breath and asked that question no one wants to ask. "How much longer do you think she has?"

The doctors turned to each other, then back to me and said, "We feel she may make it through the weekend."

Today was Friday. "So, you are saying she has forty-eight hours at best?"

The response was "Yes, at best."

I made the call that everyone was waiting for. I explained what the doctors had said and how much time she had left, in their opinion.

As a family we were not surprised because she had been with us so long, but there was still that pain of losing another loved one. No matter how old they are, it's still a loss. I called my friend Elise to let her know what was going on. She was there in two hours to help me. Once she got there, I knew I could go do the things that needed to be done.

My first stop was the nursing home to let her nursing crew know what the doctor had said. They all were upset. One of the nurses was trying to figure out how to tell the residents that this was happening. Or should they wait until she passed to let them know?

My next stop was home, to pull out her dress that she wanted to be buried in, to take to the cleaners. What is funny is, she was adamant that she be buried in the dress she wore to my wedding. Her thoughts were like my father's she spent over $80.00 for this dress she was going to take to the Lord with her. My dad was the same way. He spent $89.00 on a tuxedo rental. I was going to get married or have a funeral. You got to love them both.

From there, I went to the funeral home to give them a heads-up on what was going on. The funeral director was a family friend; he had overseen all our losses. We talked for a bit just to get an idea of what she wanted done and to see if there was still an open place next to my great-grandmother still available.

Due to the amount of time that had gone by, the plot next to her mother was used by someone else. I returned to the hospital to talk to the nurses about the hospice and the steps we needed to take going forward.

As I walked to my grandmother's room, there was a sign on the door that was too familiar to me. It was the purple butterfly, which meant comfort only. There was no need for medical help to keep her comfortable.

When I walked into the room, Elise said she had been asking for me. She heard my voice and woke up at once. That was when I had the same talk with her that I had had with my dad. I explained to her that the doctors had done all they could do this time, and we were there to make her comfortable.

Shockingly, like my dad, her response was the same. She said that she was right with the Lord, and if it was her time to go home, then she was ready. She had one request: she wanted to go back to the nursing home to die. When the doctors came in, we talked about her request. It was agreed that she could return to the nursing home on Sunday.

Hospice and I got everything together for this to happen. That Sunday morning, when she started to eat food, we were happy, but I was a bit upset because my dad had done the same thing. The morning before he died, he was up talking and eating, and he died the next morning.

With that being said, I was in more of a rush than usual to get her back to where she wanted to be. Elise was there the entire time. What a welcome she got from the staff and residents when she came back. It was like a little celebrity had come into the nursing home.

Forty-eight hours had come and gone, and she was eating, talking, and sitting up with help in her bed. Three weeks later, she was in her wheelchair moving around. My heart was full. The devil hadn't won this battle. She was back to asking for her chicken wings and snacks.

We were all shocked because according to the doctors, she was not supposed to be here. Since she was healing and bouncing back, it was time to pay the bill. I was writing the check for the month, and when I looked, I shook my head. I looked at it wrong and thought I saw an extra zero. No worries. It was now time to apply for her Medicare. They would take over now.

The stress of doing this monthly was over. I let the nursing home know that I had sent in the paperwork so that they would know that August and September would now be picked up by Medicare. We all started to focus on the turnaround that she had made. We all were so happy with this complete change of events.

October was here. I got a letter from Medicare saying that she had rejected my bank statements and receipts didn't match. Their records showed that I was off a bit of money. I needed to send them the rest of the receipts before she could get approved.

I didn't know that the nursing home had gotten the same letter. I went into the business office to let them know that there was a delay with Medicare. I needed to figure out what was wrong and why this was not adding up.

I pulled up my online banking records. My eyes widened. I sat there in disbelief. I found the error it was me; I had screwed up. How did I do this? Then I pulled up my bank statements. I was again in shock. This was a mess; I had never messed up anything this badly in my life. I had managed my mother's Medicare without any issues, so why had I made such a mess of this?

Now I have a clear head. Trying to figure it out, I guessed I would need to work two jobs and not let my grandmother know that something was going on. She was doing amazing; there were no signs that she was ever sick or near death. She was a true blessing; I would do what I could to make sure that nothing happened to her.

I went to the nursing home, and I explained to them that I had found the error and how it had happened. What would they suggest I do? Little did I know that they were out for blood not to help me help my grandmother. The nursing home was looking for $30,000 to keep my grandmother there.

I talked to the director of the nursing home, and we sat down. He could tell that I was upset and worried about my grandmother. He said that I had nothing to worry about. "Just keep getting the issue at hand fixed, and we will take care of your grandmother."

I left his office feeling much better. I could solve this problem without having to worry about my grandmother having to leave. He also assured me that they would talk to Medicare, and this would be taken care of.

We found out in November that was a lie. The first week of November, I received a letter saying that I had until December 31 to pay $43,000, or they would have to seek legal action. At this point I was a complete wreck. I took the day off to see my friend.

The office staff said she recommended that I do that promptly. "Because quite frankly, right now you look like a suspect just because there is accounted money and your trips you have taken. So you need to find the receipts or balance this out quickly."

I could have passed out right there in her office. I had no idea why this was not balancing out. As soon as I got into the car, all I could do was cry to the point of throwing up. What would I do now?

I needed a place to go to just breakdown without the kids seeing how much this was getting to me. Elise reminded me that I had done nothing wrong. I needed to focus on getting the money and not worry about what had happened to the money. Just focus on my grandmother, putting her first, and this would all work out.

That was exactly what I did. I started making every effort that I could to get the money needed to take care of my little friend. I started by getting a loan on my house. My house at the time had $250,000 in equity. You would think that would be easy, right? Not even close.

Even with the equity in the house, the big-name banks wouldn't consider the loan, even with the house as collateral. My credit score had taken such a hit from trying to get a loan that now I couldn't get a bank to look at my request. If I had a cosigner, then it wouldn't be a problem to get it down. I knew that I could get a cosigner without a problem. I had an army in my corner.

I was so devastated that all the people I had helped when I was able were now no longer returning my calls or were giving me excuses as to why they couldn't do it. The reasons I got were understandable. I had one high school friend I reached out to for help. He was going through his own battles, and I thought if we worked together, we could help each other. To know that my high school classmate and friend would help me out was so heartwarming.

He called the bank without hesitation; he was unable to help me, according to the bank. I thanked him so much for at least stepping up when others didn't. I was starting to give up all hope when a friend of mine reminded me that you never give up and you never give in.

I continued to make calls and send emails and text messages. I got a call back from a family friend who recommended someone who could work around my credit score to get this done for me.

The banker and I started to work together. Everything was going great, but we were running into the

Christmas break, which would make it harder for the banks to decide because of closing during the holidays. I was told to enjoy the holidays; we would start again on the twenty-sixth, when the banks open back up.

I let the nursing home know what was going on. My goal was to keep them in the loop during this entire process. Again, I was assured that nothing would happen to my grandmother. That made enjoying the holidays much easier.

With all that was going on with the nursing home and APS, it was still the time for giving. I was able to collect gifts from the community to share with the residents there who didn't get a Christmas gift because of loved ones who couldn't make it in.

And that was just what we did—enjoy the holidays. It was one of the best ones we had had in a while. Everyone was there, the boys. We ate, played games, and watched football. It was truly an enjoyable time. I didn't want this day to end, because I knew what tomorrow was going to bring.

It was the twenty-sixth of December, the day I was hoping would be a good one. That would not be the case. When I opened my email, there was the same response that I had received repeatedly. Now I had five days to get this done. My back was against the wall with no hope in sight.

I reached out to my realtor to see if she had any ideas or suggestions that I could go with. She had one more. It was a small bank that was only in our town, and they looked at more than your credit score. I had five days left, so I couldn't leave any stone unturned.

I met with him and got the same answer. I was beyond devastated that nothing I had done went as planned. I missed the deadline of December 31. I was not going to worry. The nursing home had said that they would take care of my grandmother. I was assured that nothing would happen to her. It was reassuring to know that I could continue to work on taking care of this mess.

2020 | APS

CHAPTER 4

SCHOOL WAS BACK IN SESSION. Time to focus on work and the problem at hand. On January 10, my phone rang. I didn't pick it up because it was an unknown number. When I listened to the message, I almost passed out.

APS was looking for me. The nursing home had turned me in. APS wanted all the documents that I had for my grandmother. If I didn't turn them in, Agent Beth would go to the police. Then she added that even if I didn't turn them over, I would be a suspect in taking advantage of my grandmother.

I called her back and explained the entire situation to her all the way up to trying to get the loan to take care of my grandmother. Little did I know that I had just given her ammunition to come after me. The next call was that I had twenty-four hours to turn over said documents, or a police report would be filed.

I called the lawyer who had helped Eric with his traffic stop. She was so helpful and understanding. Before she could talk to me anymore, she needed a $1,000 retainer fee. With all that I had spent trying to get the loans approved, I didn't have that cash on me.

I called Elise, crying on the phone about what was going on. She hung up with me, called the lawyer, and paid the retainer. The fight began. I scheduled a meeting with my lawyer, and here was where it all came to the table. I explained to her about my grandmother's near-death experience, filing for Medicare, and why it was rejected. How I was trying to get the loan to take care of the bill. How the nursing home had said she would be safe there.

She asked what had happened and why the bookkeeping error happened. That was when, for the first time, I had a real breakdown. It felt good to let that go. I sat up in the chair. I pulled out a binder with over two hundred pages of bank statements, receipts, and highlighted information. Then I began.

I buried my husband two years ago, sold my house, bought a new house, sold my grandmother's house, and moved her to a nursing home. So, I was overseeing multiple accounts and events in a two-year span. I had in the past managed my mother's Medicare without any issues at all. Everything was within $100 at any given time. So for this to be that far off, I couldn't believe it.

She began to go over the documents and could clearly see that this was a simple bookkeeping error. She could see payments that came out of my grandmother's account for my bills. She could also see in my account where my grandmother's bills were, as well as looking at my credit card statements.

When she asked me how I paid the credit card bills, I told her that I used the app on my phone to make the payments. When she looked at how I paid the bills, her reply was the problem was that the banks were in alphabetical order, and if I didn't pay attention to what button I selected, then I would pick that one. There were a couple of months when the credit card bill was paid from both accounts for the same amount.

I knew in my heart that I hadn't done anything wrong or intentional. Proving it was another story altogether. She thought we had a good chance to prove it and win if this ever went to court. I told her of my decision to put my house on the market. Since the equity was there, it could take care of everything. She agreed that it would take care of everything, but it would also make it seem as if I was guilty also.

I felt like I was in a demanding situation. She told me to continue my daily routine, and her office would take over from here. For once I felt like things were going to finally get resolved. I was wrong. When I got home, there was a warrant in debt from the nursing home for the balance due. There was also a warrant of eviction for my grandmother. She had to be out of the home by the end of January.

This was when I just felt like I couldn't take another hit on this mess. I looked at my younger son and remarked that I understand why people who are stressed out and overwhelmed take their lives. It wasn't anything that I was thinking; it was just a statement. From that point, he stayed constantly watching over me. I didn't realize that was why until I said the same thing to a coworker.

She was ready to reach the hospital to have me watched for seventy-two hours. I told her I was fine. I just understood how being stressed could take you to that side IF you had no one to talk to or help you. That was not my case. I was surrounded by friends and family members who kept me grounded.

The following week I returned to my lawyer's office with warrants in hand. She said it was time for us to add more resources to our camp. Whatever she thought was best, I was going to follow her lead. We reached out to get an ombudsman to manage all my grandmother's needs at the nursing home. She would be that go-between for all her medical needs and help her with any questions she might have about what was going on.

Next, she wanted to hire a lawyer who managed elder rights, Medicare, and APS dealing with legal issues. So here I had the dream team of elder care. I started with the ombudsman. We met to talk about what was going on and everything that had taken place.

I explained to her that I had talked to my grandmother, and she understood parts of what was going on but not all of it. She couldn't understand how someone could come after me using her money if she didn't call anyone or have any complaints about it.

She was confused by everything that was happening because she had left me in charge of everything, and she didn't feel that anyone should have anything to do with her business. Her biggest concern if something happened to me like death, who would be there to take care of her. Yes, I have a brother, but he shows up when it's needed.

The ombudsman's plan was to meet with the nursing home administration and nurse to see what her health status was and to take on the eviction notice. She assured me that if there was not a safe place for my grandmother to move into, by law they could not remove her from the facility. At my home there was nothing but stairs, and it was not wheelchair accessible.

Later that day I met with the elder lawyer. She knew her elder law and was ready to fight. She told me that I had nothing to worry about. She explained that going over the paperwork that the criminal lawyer had sent over, there were a couple of legal items that they had overlooked, and they shouldn't come after me for anything.

Before she could take the case on, she would need $3,000.00. I almost passed out in front of her. It was all I could do to get the money for the criminal lawyer, and you are saying you need $3,000.00 before you join in on this fight?

I had to come up with a plan quickly. My last resort was to go to a car payday loan place to get the money. I put my fully paid car on the line for this. My thought process for doing this was that when my house sold, I could pay everything off including the loan against this car. I had full trust in everyone who was going to bat for me.

I took the suggestion of the loan people to set aside the first payment so I wouldn't have to worry about if I had enough money to make the payment. We had people coming through to see the house, but no one would put an offer in on it. It was on the market for $50,000 less than the others in the neighborhood.

On top of dealing with all my personal issues, we were dealing with the start of a worldwide pandemic. It wasn't anything to play with. When I explained to my grandmother what was happening in the world outside her doors, she said she had seen worse, and we should not be acting all crazy. I tried not to laugh, but she was correct, over one hundred years of age, you have seen your fair share of history.

It was time to make the next payment, and I didn't have any money. I was at my wit's end. My coworker who had listened to this drama from the beginning knew I was struggling, so he loaned me the money so I could keep my car. I promised him that as soon as my house sold, I would pay him back. He understood, and he trusted me with that.

March came, and that was when things all started to change for everyone. We shut down everything due to COVID. Everything came to a complete stop. During shutdown, I picked up two little side jobs that would bring in grocery money and light bill money. I sold jewelry and candles to help make ends meet.

It helped for a while, but at least once a month, if not twice, I would have to go to the food bank because we didn't have any money to go to the store during the shutdown, and I was unable to bring in a steady check. The payday loan people didn't want to work with me. I was trying to work out an agreement with them and make smaller payments so that they would still get paid.

But the harassment continued. I didn't really understand. They knew that the entire country was in a pandemic. Why or how could you expect someone to pay the entire amount? I had gotten tired of the calls; it wasn't just a phone call a day. They would call at least three times a day if not more.

I took my car to the local car dealer, sold it, and paid off the loan against the car. I had enough to buy a sedan, navy blue, a color I had always wanted. After I got the car, our state went into complete quarantine. You could only go out if you were essential or emergency or working.

I am the type that gets cabin fever. So, I would leave to go see my friends. How did I pull this off? I would leave around 8:00 a.m. like I was working or 5:00 p.m. like I was returning home. The highways were very empty. If I was to get stopped, I would tell them that I was on my way home.

During this time, I binged on TV shows. My friends I visited had taste in food that was different from mine, so I was exposed to new shows that I would never look at as well as different foods. It was great. This was what I needed to keep my mind off the drama that was going on in my life.

COVID was starting to take its toll on everyone. I didn't know how much it was taking a hit on me until Mother's Day weekend. The restrictions were so strong throughout the state of Virginia about the contact you could have with someone. The nursing home came up with an amazing idea a Mother's Day parade.

I was so excited that I was going to see my grandmother for the first time in two months. She was outside in her wheelchair, wrapped in a blanket and bunny ears. I had to get out of the line and pull around to the back of the building. I was crying so hard that I couldn't breathe.

I called my friend Elise as always; she was amazing at calming me down. Once I calmed down, I was able to get back in line to see her. It was a great thirty-second visit. To see her as happy as she was seeing everyone driving by was amazing.

When I got home, I noticed something different about myself. I didn't understand why I was feeling so upset at everything little thing. After a full twenty-four hours of crying, I called my doctor. We had a Zoom meeting. I was able to talk to him about feeling on edge for the last month and what happened when I saw my grandmother.

I took a deep breath and explained that I was suffering from depression. I was completely shocked at the outcome of this meeting. He put me on the max of antidepressants in addition to the antidepressant that I was on and other medications.

During the shutdown, I started to spend more time on the jewelry business. I now had the time to get my business out to customers who were in the house, shopping because they were bored. I was now going to make this business grow.

The jewelry business which, by the way, was doing very well I took on the challenge of a candle business. To my surprise, that, too, was doing well. With both businesses doing well, I was able to get groceries, pay bills, and have a semblance of a normal life during the pandemic.

Throughout the pandemic, the rules on what you could and couldn't do would lift off and on. So that made for an interesting summer. My youngest son didn't leave the house. He followed all rules to the letter of the law. We learned how to use the app that delivers your groceries to you.

During this time while everyone was gaining COVID weight, I took the opportunity to work out. I was so proud of myself; I had gotten down to my pre-marriage weight. The shutdown was going great even with the world standing still.

As we approached August, I got the message that I would be returning to school to help students who didn't have internet or who had a language barrier. The rest of the students would receive learning online. I didn't mind going back to work, even on a limited basis. I would get out of the house without taking the chance of getting in trouble with the law.

I now had a timeline of what the rest of my summer would look like. I wanted to go to the beach since the restrictions had been lifted. I picked a date, and off to South Carolina I went. To go somewhere after being in the house for such a long time, to be on the beach even with restrictions, was great.

At the beach you had to make a six-foot square in the sand so that the social distance requirements were met. I spent most of the day on the beach. I was having a fun time. This was the first time that we had been to South Carolina in a while. It was a shock to see so many people at the beach.

Once COVID was over, I planned to return to this beach more often.

August came, and it was time to return to a partially open school. I still had that issue with my grandmother in the back of my mind. I knew that it would come back up at some point. It was like holding my breath every day.

As I continued to struggle with being separated from my grandmother, not being able to get out of the house like I used to, and how the world had changed, at my follow-up my doctor suggested that I start seeing a psychiatrist. With all that was going on, it was hard enough to get food on the table sometimes, so to think about giving someone $200 an hour two times a week that was not an option. When I returned to school, I started to put pen to paper. Once school started, I switched over to putting my thoughts on the computer. Each day I would add to my online journal. Before I knew it, I was thirty-five pages into it.

One of my coworkers was reading it, and she suggested that I submit it to a publishing company. I thought she was crazy, and I continued venting about my life.

I took her advice. I gave my thirty-five pages of what I had written so far, knowing nothing would come of it. I noticed that this was a strange way of making me feel better.

I continued to journal. I also picked up another relaxing hobby, coloring. Currently, coloring books for adults is a popular thing. I cannot begin to tell you how relaxing that was.

My birthday was getting closer, and I wanted to do something. I thought a nice get away would be great. Instead of spending money on a party, I would take a trip. Anyone who wanted to go with me was more than welcome. I wanted to go somewhere that had excitement, fun things to do, and tasty food.

New Orleans was my pick. I was so excited to plan my trip. I knew that my crew would be on board. I was so wrong. They had other plans at that time. None of them could go on the dates I had picked out. I changed the dates to make sure that they would be able to spend my birthday with me.

It was now the end of August, and we were starting to adapt to the new way of going to school. I was steadily plugging away at my online journal, and an email message popped up from my lawyer. The subject read "APS." My heart sank.

Scared to open the email, I let it sit for a little while before it opened it. I clicked on Open, and it read "Good morning, Pam. I wanted to reach out to you to let you know that APS needs a copy of the POA. Once that is received, your case is closed."

I started to cry. Was I reading this correctly? Was I being punked? With one simple click, this nightmare would be behind me. I scanned the documents needed for my lawyer. I sent a follow-up email to confirm that once I sent this to her, this was over.

Her response was yes. What an amazing birthday gift—this mess was over, and I could stop looking over my shoulder, wondering if every police officer I drove past would pull me over because of this mess. I was as happy as I could be.

Now it was time to really get excited about my trip to New Orleans. The good news continued to keep coming in. I got an email from the publishing company that what they had seen so far was something that would fit in their library. They wanted a completed manuscript by the end of March.

I was excited and overwhelmed at the same time. This was a venting tool for me. I never ever expected it to turn into a book. What an amazing birthday month. September was here, and now it was time to start getting my life back on track.

With bags packed, I got a call that there had been an emergency, and my friends would not be able to attend the trip planned for my birthday.

With a broken heart, I loaded the plane to NOLA to have a fun time. I was on this trip with limited money. When I checked into the hotel, they held money for pending damages—they took all that I had available. I went to my room and had a complete breakdown. I was so far away from home without money.

Once I pulled myself together, I worked up the nerve to reach out to my friend Dee and my sis-in-love. They both supported me with enough to eat and have fun. What a blessing they were. I can't begin to tell you how many beignets I ate during this trip.

I met an artist who did NOLA landscape paintings. I treated myself to one. I strolled Bourbon Street. I couldn't believe the number of stores and hotels that were closed due to the pandemic. The places that were open had the best food I had had in a long time.

Looking over my available money, I had enough to take the dinner ferry. I might have been alone, but that didn't stop me from having an amazing time. As my friends and family know, I never meet a stranger. I bought my ticket for the ferry, and I noticed a family trying to take photos. I walked over to help them get a good group photo.

While helping them, I found out that one of the sons was heading toward Charlottesville, Virginia, for a training program. We all were heading in the same direction. One of the sons asked if I knew of a place that had good beignets. That was right up my alley. We all walked to the one and only place I would go to for those tasty pastries.

I was going to leave them there to enjoy; instead, they invited me to stay with them and eat, so I did. They were having a fun time with a stranger just sitting outside listening to NOLA music playing live. I was having fun with complete strangers.

I returned to the hotel room. Since I was alone, this was a perfect time to continue to work on my book. I have noticed that when I am in a place with no distractions, I can apply myself better than when I am home with all the distractions.

Time for the ferry dinner ride. The food, music, and drinks were great. I partied with a group of people I met waiting in line. Even if you are on a trip alone, you are never by yourself. I am trying not to laugh at myself for a trip that I thought I was going to be alone on. It turned out that the only time I was alone was in the hotel room.

I returned to work; the students were excited to see me back. I enjoyed being around the students. Working with our Latino students, my eyes were opened to how similar the struggles are. I had never noticed that our Latino students were treated differently from other students until we worked together. What a wonderful group of students.

They were helping me learn Spanish. What was so funny about this was that I didn't know what I was learning until Ginger came into the room. She was like, "Pam, don't use those words" with a hearty laugh.

I turned. "Why?"

She said, "They are teaching you to cuss in Spanish."

The room erupted in laughter. I can say that this was one of my best experiences working with students.

The weather was now starting to change. It was time to get ready for winter.

It was late October. My phone rang, a local number that I was not familiar with. I let it go to voice mail. I waited until the message loaded. I started to listen to it, and I could feel the color leaving my body. My legs started to get weak. Tears were burning my face. I grabbed Ginger. I asked, "Please listen to this." As she listened to the message, her eyes started to get big.

I started crying again, to the point where I couldn't stop or catch my breath. I asked her, "What should I do?"

Her response was to call my lawyer at once. I left the classroom. All my students wanted to know if I was OK, I told them yes, I was I had to run out to do something, and I would be right back.

I was sitting in my car, never leaving the parking lot. I reached out to my lawyer, and as soon as she picked up, with tears steadily rolling, I started to say that I had gotten a call. She said, "Yes, from the local detective."

I think I dropped my phone. He had contacted her with the request that she return his call ASAP.

Why was he calling me? I thought everything was over and we didn't have to deal with this anymore. What was this? What should I do? At this point I was in full freak-out mode. Her response was that she was bound as an officer of the court to call back.

I didn't have to call back, but if I did call, don't tell him anything because it could be used against me. I had to sit in the car for a few minutes to pull myself together before returning to the classroom. Every possible scenario was going through my head.

I replied with the message: "Hello, Ms. Coleman, this is Detective McDole. We have been contacted to investigate a case of misuse of money for one Ms. Jamison. I need you to call me back at your earliest convenience to discuss this matter."

What should I do? My lawyer said not to, but I needed a second opinion. I called the lawyer who was taking care of the elder part of this. I knew she didn't manage criminal cases, but I needed someone else who knew the law to ask questions to.

I told her what had happened. She, too, said that if I called him back, all the notes he would take could be held against me. The entire time that I was in the car, he called me at least five times. Her advice to me was to call him back and let him know that I had been instructed by my lawyer not to say anything about this. I thanked her for her time.

I worked up the nerve to call. The detective answered the phone with this deep voice that scared me just to hear it. I apologized for the delay; because I worked in the school system, sometimes it was hard to get away to use a phone.

He started off by telling me that he had been contacted to escalate the investigation. "You are the prime, only suspect in the abuse of your grandmother's money. What day can you come to talk about this?"

Everything that had been told to me just five minutes ago was gone. "Why is this coming up again? I had been told that this matter was over. I didn't do anything wrong."

His response was "Let's talk about it to clear your name."

Again, everything that was told to me was GONE!

"What times do you have available? Tuesday at nine a.m. does that work for you?"

"Yes, sir, it does."

I called my criminal lawyer back to talk to her about this. She answered my questions. Then she dropped a bomb. "Pam, I cannot help you any further unless you pay $2,495.00. This is the $1,000 retainer fee and the balance that you owe."

"WHAT…wait, you can't help me?"

Her reply was "No. Not until the balance is cleared."

I hung up and lost it again. Where was I going to get that kind of money? I lost my car two times making sure that this was managed, and there was no work-around to help me out. Her response was a stern no!

"Before we hang up, I need you to not go to this appointment, along with refusing to talk to anyone without a lawyer."

Oh, she had jokes. "You are the one that has over two hundred pages of documents and paperwork to support what happened. Now you want me to start over."

This was getting to be more than I cared to manage. I went back inside and took the rest of the day off. I wasn't going to ask my plus-one to help with this amount of money. If something happened to us, I didn't want this over my head with him.

I began my search for either the money to pay the lawyer or a lawyer. After I had reached out to five different lawyers, one returned my phone call. I told him what was going on, and his reply was that he worked with both sides, as a district attorney as well as a lawyer. His advice to me was to cancel the appointment.

"Don't answer any question unless they arrest you."

He said that if I walked in to talk to him, I wouldn't walk

out. They would ask me questions to trap me, and then he

had grounds to arrest me.

At this point I needed to throw up.

The next morning, I called the detective. I told him

that I didn't feel well; this entire thing was upsetting me, and

I wasn't coming in. The pressure started. "So, when do you

think you will make it in? We need to hear from you about

what happened. Your side of the story is important to this

case if it goes forward or we close it."

I replied, "I understand. I was told by a lawyer to say

nothing, so I am not saying a thing at this time." I hung up.

I sat down to compose an email to both lawyers to let

them know what had happened. The response I got back was

so crushing. "This is the last correspondence I am having

with you. I have talked to the detective; I recommend that

you not talk to him without a lawyer present. If you are arrested, say nothing."

The elder lawyer agreed with her. The elder lawyer was so helpful and supportive. I took all their advice—I did nothing, I said nothing.

Evan and I were coming home from the store. I looked at him and said, "I understand now why people do what they do when faced with no options and no help."

If I made a statement to the detective, anything I said would be used against me. I wasn't. I understood why, when faced with so much overwhelming pressure, you would think that was your only choice. I knew if I did that, what an impact it would have on my kids and grandmother. So I had to find the strength to push through.

It is hard to always be that person who is strong, that person who lifts everyone else up. I sat in my bedroom and cried until I had no more tears left. Why is this happening to me, Lord? I have taken care of so many people. I made a mistake; I wouldn't do a thing to hurt my grandmother.

I know we must have a test to have a testimony. I didn't do well on the test, Dear Lord; I feel like I am going to fail this one. Please help me find the strength that you know I have.

The detective left more messages, and then they stopped.

If the calls stop and you have not been served, there is nothing to worry about until there is something to worry about.

We were now getting ready for Thanksgiving. I was trying to remember the things that I was thankful for and stand in those blessings and not the negatives or the what-ifs.

I began to get so excited about Thanksgiving. This was taking my mind off what was going on. I had to work at the big-box store, and my shift was 2:00–11:00 p.m. Others were not excited about working, but my plan was to turn it into breakfast and leave the dinner for the boys.

I fixed a huge breakfast. My boys and I had a fun time eating and laughing.

This was what I needed in my life. After Thanksgiving, Christmas is my all-time favorite holiday. Yes, Christmas, as we all know, I turned the inside of my house into a Christmas palooza. Everything that had gone on three weeks ago was in the rearview mirror.

While planning for Christmas, I was also planning for a New Year's getaway. Last New Year's was funny but not funny. I spent time in DC. At the last club, waiting to bring in the New Year, the alcohol began to take over. I saw New Year's come and go asleep. When it was time to return to the hotel, I left my food and drinks from New Year's Eve on the streets of Washington DC.

I wanted this one to be special. Let's focus on Christmas. The house was decorated, and the smells of Christmas were throughout the house. I was off Christmas Eve and Day. That meant I was able to stay at home and meal prep. I binge-watched every Christmas show there was on TV. All gifts were wrapped under the tree.

The little kid was coming out of me every day. Evan was hiding boxes in his room, which meant he had tried his hand at shopping. He was a good shopper when it came to getting gifts for others. This was going to be a good year for our family. This time of the year, I also missed my dad more than usual. The tears started to flow; I was missing my dad the most. He joked about my house, and he was asking for a plate of food to go.

I managed to pull myself together before Evan came downstairs. We had our dinner, which was good, and opened our gifts.

Evan returned upstairs, and I returned to watching TV. Somewhere the day had gone from pure excitement and joy to it's over to what time I must be at work tomorrow. It is sad that you put in all the work prior to Christmas day, and once the gifts are opened, the day returns to normal.

It was New Year's Eve. I had the trunk packed with amazing items. I had dinner cooked by one of my good friends who was a chef. I had steak, lobster, mashed potatoes, and spinach, which was paired with wine. It was me, myself, and I ready to bring in the New Year.

2021 | THE ARREST

CHAPTER 5

ON FEBRUARY 7, MY PHONE RANG. Any number that I didn't know, I would let go to voice mail. Once the voice mail hit, I listened to it. I couldn't believe what I was hearing. We had a family friend who had been on the police force for years, and he was on the voice mail. "Pam, it's John. Can you call me back as soon as you get this message?"

With my heart in my stomach, I called him back.

"Hey, Pam, I hate to be the one to make this call, but I'd rather it be me than someone else. Paperwork has come across our desk. I picked it up so that no one else would manage it.

"We have a warrant for your arrest. I know that you don't want us to come to the school. Is there any way that you can meet me at the magistrate's office?"

With tears in my eyes, not knowing what to do, I agreed to meet him there.

Once I got there, He explained that I was being arrested for felony embezzlement. I was about to throw up at this point. I must get into the police van.

This was for show purposes. When I stepped into the van, I couldn't move. My knees were against the door. The seat fit like a rollercoaster ride. We drove into the holding area, and he opened the door. At this point I believe I was hyperventilating; I couldn't get out of the van. I was allowed a couple of minutes to pull myself together while he did paperwork.

He reminded me that he was an officer of the court; even though we were friends, please don't say a thing to him. It was so hard to do. There was a sense of comfort that he was there, even though I couldn't say anything to him. It felt like I had someone there with me who had my back.

Once inside, the seriousness of what was going on began. "Ms. Coleman, do you know why you are here?"

"No, I do not."

"I have a warrant for your arrest. You are being brought in on charges of taking money from your grandmother—more than $10,000.00.

"At this time, you will be fingerprinted, photographed, and bond set. Since you don't seem to be a flight risk, you shouldn't have a problem leaving as soon as we are done."

I again started to get very lightheaded. I was in a place of fear in my life that no one should ever be in. I was going through this for making an error. Really?

The process began. He assured me that he was there to help me as Kevin (my late husband) would have wanted. We walked over to the fingerprinting station. It wasn't like it was back in the day with the ink pads. You now place your hand down and hold it there until the light turns green. And just like that, they have your prints.

You know how you can see something out of the corner of your eye? I turned, and there were inmates waving and hitting the glass. I threw up in my mouth a little. I am not one to judge and couldn't have cared less why they were in there.

It was the fact that I was there. I had to block them out of my view. I couldn't find a happy place to escape to—

look at where I was. I couldn't think straight, let alone find a happy place.

Time for the photos. I turned around, and I now could see them clearly.

I heard someone say, "Ma'am, please put your back to the wall and look straight ahead. Turn to your right. Now your left."

As I was turning to my left, my knees gave way. I hit the floor. All I could see was the ceiling and two police officers standing over me.

Instead of standing up, I asked if he had gotten the photos he needed. How stupid was that? I sat in the chair for a couple of minutes. Next, I was going to get bond. The only thing that was going through my mind was, I have nothing to secure this bond. What will I do if it is a crazy amount?

The only person who knew I was my coworker. I had told her that I needed to run across the street. If I needed someone to help me, who would I call? I stood before the officer, who gave me the paperwork to fill out. Everyone could see that I was shaking as I was writing.

The officer behind the glass could see that I was visibly upset. I answered all his questions. He left the window. When he returned, he gave me a laundry list of things that I couldn't do. If I didn't follow the rules set forth by his office, I would be picked up and put in jail until it was time for me to go to court.

The next thing was for him to set a court date. The date was set for two weeks from today. I agreed to all terms, and I was released on my own recognizance. As soon as I got into the car, I called my best friend of thirty years. When I told her what had just happened, she had to calm me down.

I couldn't breathe, and I had to return to work like nothing had happened. I was not going to let anyone at work know about what had taken place. I got back and told my friend. She couldn't believe everything that I was saying.

She also couldn't believe that I had come back to work. If I sat at home, I would be a wreck. The students took my mind off what had just happened.

At that time, it was hard to stay calm, when my world seemed to be crumbling around me. My court date was two weeks away; I had time to reach out to my lawyers for help. I remembered last year that my lawyer had told me that she would not help me unless the balance was paid in full. This was an emergency. She knew the entire situation; I hoped there was something we could work out so that she could take on my case.

I really didn't want to explain what had happened all over again to another lawyer. I called my criminal lawyer. Just as I expected. No, I can't help you until you pay the past-due amount and another $1,000 retainer fee. I was crushed.

She did explain that the first court date would be to decide if I had retained proper representation. I took the rest of the afternoon just to clear my mind. When my sons got off from work, I rallied them together to explain what had taken place.

My oldest was livid. We had just had the death of a young Black man at the hands of an officer. Which led to the rant my son had against the police. I explained to him that the person who arrested me was a family friend. If it wasn't for him, I wasn't sure what would have happened. My youngest sat quietly and was trying to console me because at this point, I was crying uncontrollably.

Once I calmed down, we all sat down to talk about the chain of events that had taken place earlier today. They were all in agreement that I need to find a lawyer. If I couldn't find one, I needed to go with the public defender. This was when I lost it, along with my faith in the legal system.

"A public defender," I yelled. "They don't care about me. It's a caseload for them. It's one or the other—a plea deal or conviction. I am not putting my life or freedom in their hands. Nope, not going to do it."

We ordered food to lighten the mood a bit. It was time for the plus-one to go home. I was so glad he took the time out to check on me and make sure I was doing OK.

I went to bed; I can't say that I went to sleep because that didn't happen. All I could think about were the what-ifs. What if they don't believe me that it was really a mistake? What if all they want to do is throw me in jail? What happens to my kids, my house, my job, my reputation in the community? I tossed and turned the entire night.

The sun came up, and I was still awake. I started to google attorneys who managed criminal cases, with a specialty in felony charges. I also reached out to friends who knew what was going on. I got names from them. I was armed and ready to tackle this. I got dressed and headed off to work. I couldn't let those kids down.

While the students were working, I was on the internet getting the needed information to call these lawyers. Also, I was able to send emails. This was a better choice for me than the phone. Every time I had to explain what happened, I would either break down, start crying, or get so angry and bitter that I was even going through this at all.

The entire time, I had been able to keep this from my grandmother so that she wouldn't get upset. The time had come for me to let her know what was going on. On my lunch break, I went to the nursing home to explain to her everything that had happened.

She had questions. Her main one was, if she didn't press charges, why did the police arrest me? My grandmother continued. "I gave you full control over everything. If I am here, I am OK."

I could tell that she was getting upset and worried. I promised her that everything would be OK. Would it really? Had I just lied to my grandmother? Was I going to make it through this mess?

I reached out to my brother to let him know what was going on. I was completely dismissed. My brother said he didn't know why I was making a big deal about it. "Nothing will happen to you; you always get out of trouble."

"OK, that was a mean remark. I am asking for support, mental as well as financial, and you can't give me that." So, I stopped talking to him about it.

I had two weeks to find a lawyer before my court date. No one had returned my calls or emails. I was starting to panic.

My phone rang. It was one of the three lawyers I had reached out to. His response was "Don't talk to anyone without representation. Oh, and my retainer fee is $3,000."

I think I passed out. I checked my email, and there was the response I was waiting for.

I had reached out to the lawyer who managed all the family legal documents, for our wills, POA, and home sales. It was not the email I wanted to see. In short it said, "Pam, due to the nature of this situation, we are unable to represent you. It would be a conflict of interest since we have both of you in the book of business."

Now I was down to one week left before my court date. I seemed to be hitting a wall at every turn; I wasn't sure what I should do. I took sleeping pills just to let my mind rest. I let the lawyer search and the research rest for a day to give my mind and body a rest.

Twenty-four hours went by fast, and I was back at it. This time my research was on the success rate of public defenders versus hired lawyers. It hit me that my great-niece worked in a public defender's office, and she was a public defender. I called her with all kinds of questions.

After talking to my niece, I felt better about my options if I took the public defender route. I didn't send out any emails or phone calls. I was going to wait for responses back from the ones I had sent out.

My court date was here. To say I was scared would be an understatement. My oldest son met me at the courthouse so that I would have support.

It was my turn, and the judge had two questions. One, did I understand the charges that were being brought against me? Two, had I gotten a lawyer? I responded yes sir to the first question and no sir to the second.

His response was that he was giving me three weeks to return with a lawyer ready to start the proceedings. I thanked him and left the courtroom. I was so glad that my son was there. I was shaking so badly. My son told me that he could see that from where he was sitting.

Now we were back on task. The goal was to find a lawyer or put my trust in a public defender. Over the next two weeks, I reached nothing but a dead end. Then I reached out to a lawyer who used to be a public defender. I thought it would be perfect if he took my case, he knew both sides of the law. I was feeling a sense of peace.

We talked on the phone. I had friends who had used him and were successful. For the first time in a long time, I was starting to feel like things were turning around. We set up an appointment to go over everything so that when we walked into the courtroom we would be prepared. When I got to his office, he was not there. I knocked, no answer. I called his phone. No answer. I sat on the steps of his office and cried for thirty minutes.

I went home and told my kids what had happened. I put in another call to my niece. Her response was "Pam, it's time to go with the public defender."

This was the hardest thing for me to hear—that there was no one willing to represent me and no one willing to take a chance on me for the monthly installments.

I was sitting in a house that had over $274,000 in equity, but I couldn't pull the money from that. I couldn't get a loan to make this right. I just didn't understand what was happening. As days went by, I reached out to all the people I could. I sat alone in my room, with my head in my hands. I looked up and asked God for help and guidance because this right here, that was facing me, I couldn't manage alone.

I went to sleep and awoke with a newfound peace. It was a very strange feeling—at that moment I knew what I had to do. Once dressed and ready to go to work, I called my job to let them know that I would be late. I had to run an errand before coming in to work.

I went down to the court office and completed the paperwork to get a public defender. Once that was completed, it felt like a weight was lifted off my shoulders. Three days later, I got a call from the public defender's office. I was assigned a woman to represent me.

I was off on my quest to see who was representing me. Her win-loss ratio. Other clients' reviews to see who was holding my future in her hands. She had an amazing record. That eased my mind even more.

My phone rang while I was doing this search. It was my public defender. I introduced myself to her. She asked me to tell her the entire story from beginning to present. I began with my handling of five different accounts, the stress of selling my dad's house, my mother and husband dying, selling my own home, and buying a new one while taking care of my grandmother. Then I had to sell her home to get her the proper care and a safe environment that she needed.

I had to manage five different accounts at one time. I never really paid attention to what checkbook or online accounts I used. So, I did the recap how my grandmother was in the hospital with forty-eight hours at the most to live. Once she pulled through, I had to pay the nursing home for the month of August. When I looked at the account, I thought that I saw $12,000 in her account. I knew that once I paid $10,000 for the month, there would be right at $2,000. I could now apply for Medicaid for her. I informed the nursing home so they wouldn't kick her out. I told her how they served me a warrant to remove my grandmother. I also told her about the other lawyers and the ombudsman who were involved in helping to keep her safe. I got a letter from the nursing home letting me know that the check didn't clear. I pulled up the account. There was $1,200 in it. Then I got a letter from Medicaid that said I needed to explain where $30,000 had gone.

With my lawyer's help, I was able to go through five different bank accounts. I was able to show that I paid my grandmother's bills out of my personal account. We were able to explain how the online error occurred. This was the fourth time I had to explain what had happened. No matter what they say, you always expect the worst. I was charged with felony embezzlement. They tell you to stay off Google; I couldn't help myself.

The information was so scary. It said if found guilty, the minimum was five years. The first thing that went through my mind was, what was going to happen to my kids and my grandmother if I went to jail for five years? What would happen to me? I didn't believe everything I saw on TV. But if it was anything similar, I was not strong enough for it.

Weeks went by, and my lawyer contacted me with a date. I was getting nervous all over again. I was to be in court the following week. She assured me that it was only to set an actual hearing date and to make sure I had a lawyer and understood my charges.

It seemed like I went to sleep that night, and I woke on the morning of my court date. I was so nervous I couldn't eat anything before I left. Sitting in the courtroom alone, I thought that I knew better; I had done this before and didn't mess it up. Could my doctor be correct? I had too much on my plate? Could all the multiple deaths really come into play in my misjudgment? Was I going to jail? I dropped my head and began to pray.

I thought I heard my name; the voices sounded so far off in the distance. It was my name that I heard. I stood up, a bit dizzy, but it wasn't the time to pass out. I walked to the front of the courtroom. I remember that I needed to keep my knees bent to keep from passing out.

The questions began. Do you know why you are here? Do you have proper representation? After I answered those questions, my lawyer spoke, and the DA spoke. I now had a trial date; it was four weeks away. This gave me time to get my affairs in order just in case something happened.

I returned to work. The only people who knew what was going on were my good friend who had been supporting me and my coworkers. I had to keep my day-to-day as normal as possible; this was no one's burden but my own. At work we had a training class that we took like an honor thing, saying that you would not do this and knew that you were supposed to do that. I was going along taking this course, and there it was.

If you were arrested, you must notify your employer within twenty-four hours. I dropped to the floor, close to throwing up. I sent a message to our vice principal that I really needed to talk to him.

I was comfortable talking to him, explaining what happened. Once our conversation was over, he explained that he understood what had happened. He would need to tell our principal, because that was the process. I was so scared when I was called in to the office.

The principal explained that I would have to have a Zoom meeting with him and HR. I understood and was more than willing to do what I needed to. The Zoom meeting was days later. I had to explain this story again. I knew it was her job, but I felt like I was under a spotlight. The one question she asked was, Hadn't I taken this class before? I responded that I had taken it every year except during COVID.

Then the response was, "So why did you not remember that you needed to contact us?"

My response was "I really wasn't expecting to get arrested ever. I didn't keep that information."

That was when my principal chimed in to say that as soon as I saw that part of the class, I stopped what I was doing and contacted our administration to let them know.

That was the most uncomfortable thing I had done in the school system. Everyone was polite as we ended the meeting. I felt good that we had everything on the table. I could now go about my way.

I was wrong. I got an email from the principal to come see him as soon as I could. As I walked to the office, the hall seemed two miles long. I walked in, and I could see the look on his face that this was not about to end well. I sat down, trying to stay upbeat and bracing myself all at the same time.

When you start your sentence with "I hate to have to do this..." OK, if it hurts you, then don't do it. He continued.

"I got an email from HR saying we must put you on administrative leave until future notice."

That hit like a ton of bricks. To soften the blow, I was on paid leave.

What would happen now? The biggest thing for them was that I didn't tell them when it took place. Not that it happened—just that I was viewed as withholding information. I called Evan to let him know what the principal's and HR's decision was. I had to turn in my school keys, badge, and laptop. I was upset at first, then I turned it into a positive.

There was so much that I needed to get done at home, to prep for the trail. I was going to take this time to get myself together, to focus on myself. I wanted to clean the garage, which seemed like a project that never ended. I wanted to pull all my clothes out of the closet oh, the list was endless.

It took me about a week to get out of the slump that I was in being put on administrative leave. Eight days in, I was ready to take on my projects. When the phone rang, it was the school.

They were happy to inform me I could come back to school. There was a stipulation: if I was found guilty, I would be fired. OK, I will take that for now. The same day I returned to work; I got an email from my lawyer that they had moved my court date out another month. I started to get nervous.

I asked her what was going on. She said the longer the DA took, the better we would be for plea deals, reduced charges let's just let them have that. I agreed. I now needed a getaway. I booked a hotel by the beach, just to relax. No matter how hard I tried, I couldn't take my mind off what was going on. I needed to focus on getting my book edited and out for all to read.

I got back on Monday to an email. When I went to court, the DA would have a proposal for me; no jail would be involved. I needed to have a Zoom meeting with her to prepare for what was going to happen in the coming weeks. I also informed her about what had happened with the school. This was the start of a good day. As I continued through my emails, there was one from the principal requesting a meeting with him and the vice principal. I was excited about this meeting; I had talked to the vice principal a while back about going to a different job in the school where I would work more closely with the students.

I accepted the meeting invitation. It was for the next morning, so I was preparing to have my strengths ready to show as to why I was the correct person for the job. Morning came, and I was standing in the office with a huge smile. This was my opportunity to be great. I walked back to the conference room and sat down.

I was asked if I knew why I was there.

I responded, "I hope you are going to tell me that I am getting the in-school suspension job."

The response knocked the wind out of me. "No, we have you here on a complaint."

WHAT!

They said that one of my coworkers came to them to express that I was not being professional in the workplace. Again, WHAT! She told them that I told her to open the "fucking" door.

Here again, I stood before someone fighting for something I hadn't done. What was going on here? I explained that I knew she was having a sad day, and I wanted to show her a funny cat video. I asked her to hurry up and open the door. It wasn't like I didn't have enough going on in my own personal life, but for someone who has attended your birthday parties, you talk to about things that others didn't know about, it really hurt my feelings. I am sorry, but I was wearing a mask and talking through a glass door; you couldn't have asked me what I said.

Since I couldn't remember 100 percent what I said to her, the principal's response was "I hate to do this."

Oh, please don't start that mess again. I ended up getting written up, and I had to apologize to her. This was complete madness. And did you want me to work in the same department as her when I return to fully working next school year? I don't think so. I apologized to her. Before she left the meeting, I asked her that if it was not related to the library when she returned next, please don't address me.

She agreed and left. I left that meeting so angry I couldn't see straight. I had been with this school system since 2009, when my first child came through here. You know that is something that I wouldn't say to someone. I wouldn't say it in the workplace. I was going to put in for jobs elsewhere, but I was doing it out of anger.

The more I thought about it, I was leaving this school one way or another.

Then my phone rang. It was my lawyer to remind me that I had to be in court in the morning. She wanted me to get there a little early so that she could go over the paperwork. Now I went from being angry to being scared again. The way things had been going for the last few weeks, this didn't seem like it was going to go in my favor either.

I got up early and struggled with what to wear to court. It wasn't like I was going on a date, so why was it so important? I settled on a subtly colored dress that went all the way to the floor. I parked in the parking garage, a walk that was a block away; it seemed to be five blocks. I got to the steps of the courthouse. I stopped to look up to the skies.

I asked my daddy to please walk through these doors with me. Stand with me as I go through this.

I asked God to know my heart, to know that I would never do anything intentional to my little granny. I dropped my head and started to walk up the steps. At the top of the stairs was my lawyer, and we went into the courtroom together. I could feel the blood leaving my body. She sat next to me. I was handed a sheet of paper to go over. I asked her if this was correct, and she said it was.

The DA's proposal was that I deposit $250 every month in an account set up for my grandmother until June of next year without any withdrawals, and all charges would be dropped. I signed that piece of paper, looked up, and thanked my daddy for walking with me.

Then I heard my name called. I walked up to the judge's bench slowly, still scared. Anything could go wrong from the time I stood up to the time I got to his bench. Oh no here comes that uncontrolled shaking again.

The DA began to speak. "Your Honor, we are here for felony charges brought against Ms. Coleman. Collaborating with her lawyer and talking to Ms. James and the nursing home, we feel that Ms. Coleman didn't act with ill intention toward her grandmother.

"Talking with Ms. James, Ms. Coleman is the only one that she wants to manage her affairs. Ms. James also said that she had not wanted anything; she had not gone hungry. When she asks her granddaughter to bring her something, she provides it without hesitation. Also, when the charge is alleged, Ms. Coleman had her husband's benefits in her account, so there was no need to take from Ms. James. What we have here is more criminal negligence, due to the number of deaths that she has had, and all the financial burden placed on her.

"If it pleases the court and Your Honor, we would like to enter this document that would extend trial until June of next year. If Ms. Coleman has not lived up to her end of the deal, then the DA's office will go ahead with full prosecution under the law."

The courtroom and all parties got extremely quiet. Then the judge spoke. "Ms. Coleman, because of the statements given by the DA and your lawyer, I will grant this request. To your lawyer and the district attorney, this is the last year-long extension of a court case I will grant you. I need you both to find another way to resolve your cases without trying up our judicial system for a year."

I was the last person called in the courtroom. It felt like forever. Before I left, my lawyer reminded me that I had thirty days to show proof that I had set up the account for my grandmother. This account had to be in her name, and she would reach out to me prior to the thirty days to make sure that it was completed.

Every deposit slip must have a date stamp on it no later than the last day of the month to count as that month's deposit. I mentally recorded everything. My lawyer saw the look of distress on my face. She assured me that this was going to work out. She would email me the directions to what was needed.

When I returned to school, I gave copies of the court outcome to my principal. He had a small smile on his face and responded, "Glad to have you with us another year."

Wait…what, really? Did you just say that you were glad but didn't have a problem writing me up? I flashed the fake smile, went back to my little workspace, and began to apply for jobs.

Within two days of hitting Enter, I got a call from the elementary school asking when I would have time to do an interview. I was so happy, I set it up for the next day. I was interviewing to work with kids with special needs. This was great, I thought. I would really be firsthand with the students, and they were small students also. This would be amazing.

I had to go through the entire weekend before I found out that I had the job. It was nice to hear that they wanted to offer me the job while we were on Zoom. It felt great going somewhere that I knew I was wanted and needed.

I know this was wrong of me, but I didn't tell them I wasn't coming back. Once the principals talked, they should know I was not coming back. I dropped off my computer again with a smirk on my face, just like a little kid—I know something you don't know. I dropped my kids at the front desk and walked out, never to look back. You know the old wife's tale: never say never.

With all that I had going on with the court system, I didn't dare take a vacation. I was missing going on a trip, but

I must push through. So the entire summer I worked to the point where I was looking forward to going back to school just to rest. Every other weekend I would work two twelve-hour shifts, on Saturday and Sunday, just to help keep the stock up.

Working during the summer, I didn't even realize how fast it went by. It was now August, time to start the new job. I was just like a little kid. I got a new backpack and lunch bag, and my hair looked super cute. I knew that I was working with special needs, but it had been left out of the interview that I would be working with severe, profound nonverbal. I was not going to run from this job; it was like family here. The people working at the school when both of my sons attended were still there. So the adjustment I would have to make was how to oversee the students.

The first day of school was here, and you could tell by looking at me that I was like a deer in headlights.

As the students were getting off the bus, I said how cute the students are.

One of the teachers said lovingly, "Don't say that."

I thought I had done something wrong.

She said, "Wait for it."

I watched the little one that I said was cute. She was walking like she was on the runway. I had to laugh; I told the teacher I understood now.

The first week was an adjustment time for me. I had to learn how to respond—when to duck a child's swing, and always remember never to turn your back. As I started to understand the job and learn my routine, my back started to act up. I felt like I was letting down the team. They assured me that I wasn't. My heart was telling me differently. I continued to push through; the pain continued.

It was the end of October, and I couldn't even lift a child or help them up off the floor. I was in so much pain. I asked for a meeting with our vice principal. We had a long talk, and she told me that if I could hold on another week, she thought she had a solution.

She did have a solution. There was another special education class in the building for older children, which didn't require the amount of lifting that I was doing. Like me, there was another young lady who had requested to be moved to another classroom setting.

Our vice principal asked me if that would be OK. I thanked her and waited for her to talk to all the people involved in this change. Two weeks later I was in a new setting. It was hard for me to walk outside to do the after-school parent pick up to see my old coworkers and friends.

To ease the separation from them, I would go back to eat my lunch in the classroom and would go see the kindergarteners I had grown attached to. As time went on, working with my new group, I started to feel like I was not part of the group. I would walk into the team meeting and greet all those there, but no one would respond.

This was not something that I was used to working with, but the primary office had just gone through all that it did to help me get a better working environment. I didn't want to go back and say this was not working. I will continue to push through, looking forward to the upcoming holiday breaks. Thanksgiving again was another holiday that I had to work this year; I didn't put effort into Thanksgiving it. I was still in a financial bind from all my legal issues.

I spent Thanksgiving with Granny. I noticed that she was starting to forget stuff. When I brought it up to the nurses, they wrote it off as her being over a hundred. I didn't agree with that answer. I could see a change in her, and it didn't have anything to do with her age. She still had a good appetite for her chicken wings, so that helped me a little bit not to worry about her too much. We talked about Christmas; I told her that I would start decorating soon.

Once the turkey was put away, it was time for me to take out the decorations. Whenever I start to feel down during the holidays, as soon as I put up the tree, everything seems to make me feel better.

For the last three years, I had had a New Orleans theme on my tree. This year would not be different.

The colors were bright and beautiful. Seeing them on the tree always made me smile. Christmas was not the only thing that I had to look forward to this year. My book was going to be released on Granny's birthday. I had to channel levels of excitement. This was a good thing for me, and I needed to celebrate it. I held it at one of our local restaurants. My friend who took our family photos was going to be there. This was going to be a good day. There was an outpour of friends there to support me, to lift me up with love, laughter, and good times. I felt really blessed, and only two of them knew what was going on outside of my boys. This was a success.

I was looking forward to Christmas. There were gifts under the tree. I was looking forward to seeing the kids as they unwrapped their gifts. Every holiday we spent together, the more it kept my mind off the fact that I was labeled a felon in the eyes of the law.

2022 | CLOSURE AND DEATH

CHAPTER 6

THE NEW YEAR WAS HERE. My goal was to have a wonderful year. To be positive, set goals for myself, and be the best version of myself that I could be. I was starting this year with a timeline for my publishing company. I had just released one book, and the other one was set to be released on my birthday. I returned to work. Seeing that the gifts I had given my team were still there, pushed into a corner, made me feel less wanted on that team than I did before we left for Christmas break.

When I saw the gifts that I had put thought into for them pushed into the corner and the non-conversation thing continued, I knew it was time to go to the office for a talk about what would be the best route to take to keep everyone happy. I got sick. I was at home for a week. During this time, I was in contact with our administration department. I told them that I would not return to work until we had a solution to the problem.

My old team checked in on me, to see how I was doing. My current team didn't check in on me. The only thing my team leader wanted to know was when I was coming back in. Two weeks later, I returned to school to have a meeting with the lead teachers. During this meeting,

I was able to express how I felt and why I didn't think this would work. During this meeting, the lead teacher was short and nasty, and she had an attitude. The principal noticed it. As the meeting concluded, she asked me if I wanted to go back to the team or return to my original. I didn't have to respond at that moment, but I knew this would be the last time they would see me unless it was in the hallway.

The next day I was reunited with my original team. I was welcome. That was what I missed. We didn't have to be best friends; all I wanted was communication in the workplace. Having communication on a team helps the kids as well as the coworkers.

Everything finally was going in the right direction. Or was it? Working as a TA in the school system, you are not making any money. It looked like every day, something was past due or was set to turn off. With the charges hanging over my head and my credit score now in the poor range, I couldn't get a loan from my house to get everything caught up. I was now back in the food bank line every other week to make sure there was food in the house.

When I went to visit my grandmother, I didn't let her know that I had hit tough times as badly as I had. I made sure that on every visit, she got her chicken wings. If she called me for something, she never had any idea that I might not have it. My lawyers told me that since I had signed over her Social Security check to the nursing home, I could ask the nursing home to reimburse me for what I got her. But with all that they were putting me through, I would not ask them for a thing.

My sons were keeping me going and reminding me that we had seen worse before and made it out. With my sons' support, I started researching my options.

As I was working on ways to get my financial issues back on track, I did my first book festival in Richmond,

Virginia. I was excited and nervous at the same time. I was learning so much from the other authors, who have been doing these events longer than I.

I got to tell people my story and why I drafted the book. It was an opportunity for the shoppers to preorder my next book. I was so happy that I sold three books. To make a sale, to meet new people. I had two people from home to support me, Elise and Rach. Rach was there to take photos of my first book festival. She always makes sure that all my notable events are documented. I am glad to have her in my corner.

I tried extremely hard to keep my bills on track and get everything caught up from my legal issues. I had to ask for help. I filed chapter 13 to keep everything that we had. Every time you think that you can't get any lower, there's always something that comes along and pulls the rug out from under you. When you file chapter 13, you get to keep everything because you are paying everyone back at 100 percent. In addition to paying $250.00 a month to stay out of jail, I now had $300.00 taken out of my paycheck every two weeks.

I was trying not to worry too much about it until I had to. I needed to stay focused on meeting my book deadline and ensuring I was making the court-ordered payments. Those payments were incredibly stressful. I had times when payday would fall on the last day of the month. That would make the date stamp show the next day or sometimes even two days later. When that happened, I would email a copy of the deposit slip to my lawyers ASAP. I didn't want the DA to think that I was not following the instructions as listed.

As I walked into work, I noticed that the TA employees were upset. I asked my coworker what had happened. She turned to me; the school board would not pay the ten-month employees year-round anymore. We would not get a paycheck in the summer. I started to stress out. I had a book deadline I had set for myself. I had a house to take care of, a grandmother to take care of, and now chapter 13 to pay, and you were telling me I would not be getting a paycheck for 2.5 months? I had 2 months to figure out what I would do.

This was enough to make me go crazy. I was so thankful for my son. He said that he would pick up the mortgage payments to make sure we wouldn't lose the house. I didn't want to put that on him, but I really didn't have a choice.

I knew this was going to be tight for the next five years, but it was what I needed to do for our household and family. You know the rainbow doesn't ever last long.

I needed to finish this school year strong and on a positive note. It was time for our school's annual field trip.

With special needs kids, this was a bit harder than a usual field trip. I had never worked with kids at this level, so I was a bit nervous. The nerves quickly went away when I saw the smiles on the students' faces. They might not be verbal, but they had ways to communicate.

It was pure joy to see them interact with their classmates. The school had our local fire station come over to spray the children with a water hose. I made it clear that I was not going to get anywhere near that water hose. My team took one for me. I was standing on the sidewalk with the kids as they took one at a time to enjoy the water. As I stood there talking to one of the medical staff that goes with us for certain children, I wasn't paying attention to where the water hose was spraying.

I was hit and hit hard. I couldn't figure out why I couldn't see. The water had knocked my glasses off. I was looking for my glasses. Meanwhile, everything and everyone was fuzzy. I thought I had one of my kids' hands. Nope, I had someone else by the hand, and I didn't know it until I put the glasses back on. Once I noticed that I had the wrong child, panic set in, but only for minutes. I looked up, and my student was in the water having the time of her life.

Spinning and dancing, she just wanted to be in the spray of water. With her as happy as she was, she needed to get out of the water. Ms. Coleman was soaked and not happy. This didn't go well at all. When I tried to get her out to the puddles of water, she hit me with a closed fist. I lost my breath and hit the ground. My coworker was on it. She grabbed her before she ran off, and the medical team pulled me out of the water. I was ready to go home. This was all I could take for the day.

As soon as we got on the bus to head back to school, my concern was not with the fact that I was soaking wet nor the fact that I was just punched in the chest. My concern was how soon my beautician could see me to get my hair fixed. Vain? Maybe. I do not like to do my hair. I was in luck. She had an appointment as soon as I got off from work.

Two weeks later I went to the ATM to make my last court-ordered payment. This was a bitter moment; I had made it an entire year making this deposit without missing one or being late. I had made all the payments with very few people knowing what my struggle was. Now the time was here to find out if the DA would stick to what was said a year ago you make these payments on time, send a copy of the deposit slip and a quarterly statement, and the charges will be dropped.

I reached out to my lawyer to see if she could ease the fear that something else would happen when I walked into the courtroom. She said that everything was going to be fine. "In two weeks, meet me outside the courthouse, and we will go over everything."

I shared with her that I was nervous that something was going to happen and that I would have to do something else to prove that I didn't mean to make this mistake.

Again, she said that the DA had all intentions of dropping the charges. "I just need you to stay calm and show up on time."

June 3 was here. It had been an entire year since I had walked into this building. I prayed to God that I would never ever have to walk into this place again. This time was much different than the last. Everyone revolving around my case was smiles. Laughter and polite conversation was going on.

I was sitting in the courtroom damn near ready to pass out, and we had good times going on. UGH! My lawyer made her way in my direction. She had a stack of papers with her—my book with the two hundred pages of documents, along with a letter and paperwork from the DA that everything was satisfied, that I had followed our agreement to the letter, and all charges would be dropped effective June 3, 2022.

I believe I sat there and cried until I heard my name called. This time I was not the last one in the courtroom to go before the judge.

The DA had his say first. He was supportive of the work I had done to keep everything on track. He remarked how I had never missed a payment and had sent in the required paperwork. He would like to drop all charges.

The judge then turned to my lawyer to see if she agreed or disagreed. Of course she agreed.

Then the judge directed his attention to me. In my mind all I could say was "Aw, shit."

"Ms. Coleman."

"Yes, Your Honor."

"I would like to commend you for following the requirements of your agreement. I understand that this has been difficult for you and your grandmother. I also understand, talking with the DA, that your grandmother has no problems with you overseeing her money because she hasn't gone without anything she wanted, and you are taking excellent care of her."

I replied, "Yes Your Honor."

"As of June third, all pending charges against will be dropped. Ms. Coleman?"

"Yes, Your Honor?"

"I hope to not see you in this courtroom again," he said with a small smile across his face.

I replied that the only time he would see me would be if we bumped into each other at the grocery store. The group laughed. I got my paperwork and headed straight to human resources.

This was a wonderful day in so many ways. I was able to keep my job in the school system, and this dark and horrible cloud was no longer over me, I could finally go into the nursing home without feeling like a criminal when I visited my grandmother. My next stop after that was to head straight to Granny to let her know what had happened.

I went into the nursing home, excited to share the news and update Granny that this mess was finally over. When I got to her room, she was sitting in her wheelchair in the sun taking a nap. I called out to her, and she woke up. My happiness turned to sadness quickly. She moved the wheelchair to face me, and she asked who I was.

I continued to talk to her so she could recognize my voice. After fifteen minutes, it came to her who I was. I told her what had happened in court today. She didn't remember what had been going on. I did my best not to cry.

The nurse came in. She said I needed to get used to it because she was over a hundred years old, and this was going to happen.

I left her room so angry that they continued to say she was old and for me to suck it up. I returned to work, relieved that this was over. I still needed to figure out how I was going to make that chapter 13 payment with no paycheck during the summer. There was one week left of the school year. I need a break, but there was no time to rest. I had my second book to release. I struggled so much to get past the first chapter that it put my entire timeline behind.

With $600 due within thirty days, what was I to do? I put in applications for a summer job. I got a job working as a salesperson for a ladies' store. I really enjoyed the people I was working with. They brought me in at a rate that was not like the others, which allowed me to keep up with the payments for chapter 13 and my court order.

I really enjoyed working at this store. My favorite thing to do was to work on the boxes when they were delivered. I got to see all the new stuff that was coming in before the other employees and customers. There were so many cute outfits I wanted to get, but I knew I had that bill hanging over my head. Spending money on things I didn't need was not an option. There was a time when I was working seven days a week to make sure that I got the number of hours needed for the $600.00. My son was a twelve-month employee at the school, so he had to go to work at 8:00 a.m. every day. There were times when I didn't have to clock in until 9:30 a.m., so while I waited to clock in, I would sit in a coffee shop working on my book.

I was so happy that I was getting the book back on track. I was feeling great about meeting my deadlines. One morning I was checking my emails, and there was one from the publisher that there would be an opportunity to travel to Texas, Illinois, and Georgia. How exciting would it be to get more exposure and more opportunities to gain experience, grow, and be the best me that I could be. I had something positive to look forward to.

I couldn't believe that August was here, and I had not seen one beach this summer. I reached out to my friends to see if they wanted to spend the day at the beach. Everyone had something else to do and wouldn't be able to join me. At first, I thought about not going, but I quickly changed my mind. I needed this break, if only for one day. I took off the following Friday and headed to the beach. I got there at 8:00 a.m. and didn't leave until a storm started to come in.

On my way home, my phone rang. It my old school. The job that I was doing with her during the COVID pandemic was available, and they wanted me to come back to the school. As soon as I got home, I put in for the job. Then I got a Zoom interview and had to wait through the entire weekend to find out if I got the job. On Monday, my phone rang. It was Ginger stating that I was wanted at the school, but my current principal had blocked the transfer. I was so upset. I really enjoyed working with the students in her class.

I got a call days later informing me that I needed to hold tight and let the schools work it out. That was what I did. When all was said and done, the high school won the battle. My principal could not block a raise and promotion. She could block a lateral move, and I couldn't take the job. It was like a homecoming, I got to see all the people I had worked with for three years again. It just felt right to return to the school.

When I got there, I just wanted to make my old coworker feel uncomfortable about what she had done and how I had left because of it. As the weeks went on, I couldn't continue to do that. She spoke to me, and I returned the hello. The next week, I stopped in to tell her about the book, and that was when she told me of her losses, pending divorce, and her mom moving in with her.

Talking to her was like nothing had ever happened, I still remembered what happened. But forgiveness is for me, not her.

Granny was still not doing well in my eyes. Everyone else was writing it off as she was over a hundred. I was so tired of hearing that. On September 8 I stopped by to see her. This time she knew who I was when I walked through the door. She asked me to sit down. She wanted to talk to me. So, I sat down. She began to tell me that she was getting tired. She didn't know why she had been here on this earth so long. The next thing she asked me to do was to clean out her room so that when she died, there wouldn't be much to take out. I started to cry but did as she wished. This brought back memories of my mother.

I had two family members die in September's past. I couldn't get that out of my mind. I was being selfish; all I could think about was, why is everyone dying in September? This was my month, my birthday month. I told myself that my mother's unhealthy habits were starting to show. I hadn't acted like her in such a long time. Now was not the time to begin.

I had a girls' getaway planned, and I could see she was starting to decline. She was eating less, sleeping more, and retaining water. I promised her that I would be strong, and whatever she wanted, I would do. She reminded me that she had had a good life and I shouldn't shed tears unless they were tears of joy. It was a hard promise, but I made it.

I loaded my car up with all the things she didn't want in the room with her, got her fried chicken, and dropped it off.

I was going to keep my promise no matter what, so I continued to plan my getaway with my girls. This was going to be a fun trip; I had worked hard to make sure that the ladies would have a fun time. The plan was to go to northern Virginia. Twelve ladies were expected to attend. I had goodie bags for the ladies, and we were to paint my room that Friday night. There was adult entertainment on deck and then Uber to the club. I requested the club to a table for me. It was $350 to get the private table, and my trusty photographer was to take photos.

The closer we got to the weekend, the confirmed ladies started to drop off, unable to come. I was appreciative of the ones who called me. I wasn't upset that they couldn't make it. They respected me enough to let me know.

I was like a little kid in a candy shop the closer we got to that Friday. I had the car packed, and when 2:00 p.m. came around, I was ready to go. I wanted to get there before the ladies who were coming in on Friday and set the room up for the painting night. Something always happens. I was delayed, two hours late leaving to head to northern Virginia. I sent a text to let them know that I was running behind.

I was thirty minutes away from the hotel when I got a text that they were there and going to get something to eat. I stated that I was thirty minutes away from the hotel, but they were hungry. I thought that would give me time to get the room together. After I put the room together, everything was set up with the drinks and snacks. I noticed that it was now 9:30 p.m. I sent a text to make sure everyone was OK. They were at a bar and said the music had just started and to come over.

I declined. I was looking at the setup, and my feelings were hurt. I sat there and painted alone. I got up the next day, went to watch the sun rise, and pulled myself together. This was my birthday weekend; I was here to have fun, so let's do that. When I returned, they had eaten breakfast. I texted one of the ladies and asked her to come to the room. When she got there, I explained my feelings. I told her that I was not paying $350.00 for a table tonight if we were not going to go. Nothing I had planned for us to do and have fun, we were doing. She agreed and told me that after they took a power nap, we would go out and do the stuff I had planned.

I fell asleep also. I woke up and texted the crew no reply. At this point I was done. I cleaned the room up and got in my car to head to the shopping outlet. The $350.00 that I was going to spend at the nightclub, I was about to drop on myself. Happy birthday to me.

As I was leaving out of the parking lot, they texted me. I invited them to go with me to the outlet. They all needed to take a shower. OK, see you all later. I had a wonderful time shopping. I found the purse that I was looking for at over 50 percent off, and other things I didn't need. But it was my birthday.

I returned to the room, filled the ice bucket, and had started to sip on peach Crown Royal when I received a text from my friend who was the adult entertainment. He was stuck in traffic and would be there shortly. I let the ladies know that he was delayed. There was a knock on the door. It was the ladies. I was sharing with them how I was feeling about all that I had put into the weekend. To be dismissed hurts my feelings. I was told to let it go—we were here now.

I believed that the very moment the old me came back, I kept my glass full. When my friend arrived, I couldn't tell you the number of shots that I had taken. Once the show started, I started to count my shots. When the show ended, I was nineteen shots of Crown Royal and Patron in.

Now we were going to the casino. I was still feeling OK, until I sat down to put my shoes on and the room started to spin. I have learned one thing from my years of drinking: you lie there and embrace the spin. Do not go in the opposite direction, or you will throw up.

I explained to the crew that I needed an hour for this to calm down, and I would be good to go. What they didn't know was that I could hear their entire conversation. They left me, went out, and had a fun time. I was up looking at TV when they returned to tell me how much fun they had. I told them that I was OK after an hour. The remark was that I should have taken an Uber over to hang out with them. I thought you all were here to hang out with me.

Still don't get it. I asked the final question: Are you all going to the museum tomorrow? Our tickets were time stamped, and we needed to be there by 12:30. Everyone was ready to go to the museum. Next morning, my only request was for the ladies to put on the outfits they had worn last night so we could get photos. Only one came upstairs. It was

11:00 a.m., time to check out, and only one was downstairs ready to go. The others asked for a late checkout, which was for 1:00.

I knew then that going to the museum was out of the question. I drove home in tears, hurt and angry. I had taken time to research stuff for us to do and have fun. Next year, I was going back to New Orleans by myself, like I always did.

That Sunday I stopped to check in on Granny. The nurses told me that she had been saying throughout the weekend that she was tired and ready to go home. I thanked them for the information and walked into Granny's room. She just looked so sad.

She told me also that she was tired and ready to leave. She didn't understand why the Lord had kept her here this long. I gave her a hug and returned home. As I worried about her, I was thirty days away from heading to Houston for a book festival. My heart was telling me that she was shutting down. If she was going to die, she was going to die when I was not in the state of Virginia.

The hospice visits increased. Their visits had been once a week; they were now going to see my grandmother twice a week. I was told it was for precaution, but I knew better. I contacted the sister-in-law to let her know what was happening. With each visit I could see a change in my grandmother. Each week I would get a call that she had fallen. It was breaking my heart that she was down to skin and bones; I knew that she couldn't take too many falls to the floor.

Granny thought that she could still transfer herself from the wheelchair to the bed, which was not the case. She wouldn't call the nurses for help. She was still determined to do things herself.

It was a week away from leaving. My visit with Granny was not the same. She was in a wheelchair, asleep. I called out to her; she had a hard time waking up.

I called one of the nurses to see if this was something new that she was doing. They responded yes. I was also informed that she wasn't eating; she just wanted her coffee. I knew at that moment that she was preparing herself to die.

I told my sister-in-law that she wasn't eating, just drinking coffee. It looked like she was eating snacks, but I wasn't 100 percent sure. She visited Granny later that day and got her to eat chicken and green beans. After hearing that, I felt better about leaving.

It was Wednesday, time for me to leave. Before I left, I had to check on Granny one more time. Today she was looking frail and slumped over in her wheelchair, over her heater. Her room was hotter than it had ever been. I checked the temperature in the room, it was set at ninety-two degrees, and she had on a sweater and a blanket. At that point I was getting prepared.

She finally woke up, and we chatted for a little bit. I didn't tell her that I was going to Texas. If she knew that I was going out of town, she would worry. I gave her a big hug and a peck on the forehead and told her I would see her soon. Her reply was "I will be here unless the Lord sees fit to finally answer my call."

On my way out, I stopped by the nurse's station to let them know what was going on. I shared my thoughts with them about her dying.

One of the nurses said, "Don't say that. It's not time for her to go."

I said, "She will die while I am gone so that I won't have to worry about her. That is what we do I tell her not to worry about me, and she will tell me, don't you worry about me."

We would laugh at each other. This time was different. I could feel it.

I was on my way to Texas. It was a good flight; I was able to work on my book and fix the issues I had with it. I was in the hotel room trying to figure out how I was going to eat and get snacks without a car.

My phone rang, and the number that came up was hospice. I took a deep breath and answered.

They were calling to tell me that Granny had fallen again. Hospice wanted to get an x-ray of her hip because she was complaining about pain. My grandmother would never say she was in pain unless she was. Hospice wanted to keep me updated on what was happening, and they would call me when they had more information.

I looked up. I said, "If this is your will, Lord, I accept it. Please wrap her in your arms and keep her safe."

I checked on Granny off and on for the next two days. Friday she was not getting out of bed, along with refusing all food and drinks. I called the hospice and explained that she wasn't going to be here much longer. Again, no one believed me.

It was now Saturday. I was at the book festival packing up my stuff. The phone rang hospice. She was putting my grandmother on morphine. When you hear "morphine," you know that this is a comfort measure.

She put the phone to my grandmother's ear, and Granny asked me when I was coming to see her. I told her that I would be there soon. I could hear her in the background as I talked to the hospice, Granny made a statement that stayed with me the rest of my trip.

"That's it no more company, I want to rest."

When I hung up, I tried my best not to let anyone see that I was tearing up. I couldn't hide it. My wonderful publishing family was there. It was a rally to make me feel better. I explained that she was 108, she was ready to go, and I must find the strength to let her go.

Still, it was hard. I knew it, I understood it, but my heart was breaking. At the same time, I was getting the information from the nurses. I got a text message that Evan had made it to Texas safely. He had come to Texas to hang out with his mom.

Evan had the restaurants ready to go that he wanted to try. We had a good pulled pork and bisque dinner. I had never seen smokers so big in my life. I guess what they say is that things are bigger in Texas.

It was twenty-four hours since I had heard from the nursing home or hospice. No news is good news. It was time to return home. Still nothing. When we landed in New York, I turned my cell phone on to see if anyone had called and to play a game on my phone. What a relief no one had called.

Just as I was putting my phone back on airplane mode, it rang. It was hospice. She wanted to let me know that Granny was now actively dying.

I sat there for a minute. I thought I had heard her correctly. I asked if she could say that again.

"Your grandmother is actively dying. She will still be here by the time you get home. We give her twenty-four hours; a week at the most."

I don't think I said too many words after that. I told her that I would call her as soon as I landed in Virginia and headed home. The last part of our trip was a forty-five-minute flight. I was home within two hours of the call. I didn't head to the nursing home; I didn't think that I could take seeing her like that. I have seen enough people leave me; that final picture stays with you. It takes a while to not see them when you close your eyes to go to sleep.

Evan asked if I was going over there, and I said, "No, I can't do it right now. I will go in the morning before I go to work."

The longer I sat in the chair watching TV, the more I felt like I needed to go over there. Evan was leaving to get something to eat and told me, "Come on. You would not feel right if you didn't go and something happened to her."

When I got to her room, she was breathing like normal a little slow but still breathing. I sat next to her, holding her hand. I said to her, "Little friend, you finally got the call that you have been waiting for. You can now answer it. You can go home now."

Granny took a deep breath, exhaled, and was gone.

My protector of fifty-six years had left me. She had always been there for me, to make sure nothing happened to me when I was in my mother's care. To make sure that I had money when I was in college. We went through deaths together, like best friends. Now she was gone. It took me a while to put the pieces together, but I got it.

On June 3, all the drama with the nursing home, the APS, and the arrest stuff had finally ended. Four months later, she was gone. She had wanted to know why she was still here; it was to make sure I was OK.

I am OK, and now she is OK. We kept our promise to each other to make sure that we were OK. She did that until her last breath. The nurses said she waited for me to come back to know I was OK before she died. I, too, believe that was what she needed to know to be at peace.

I often wondered why I never made the deadlines I set for this book. It was because the final part of the story had not been written. Now it had an ending.

I cleaned out her room and shared her things with her floor mates. Everything was put into bags for the nursing home to share with those who might need something. Trash was by the trash can. Everything that I would like to have of hers was in a bag in my hand.

I walked to the door, stopped, and turned for a last look. Here I stood in this empty room, eyes filled with tears. She's gone, she's gone was all I could say to myself. Thank you, Granny, for everything you did for me as a child, young adult, adult. Love you much, girlie.

I turned to the door and reached for the switch to turn the lights off. Her room went dark, just like the small hole in my heart. I closed the door. At that moment I knew my life would never be the same.

ABOUT THE AUTHOR

BORN TO ALFRED AND SHIRLEY JAMES, Pamela James Coleman was raised in Charlottesville, Virginia. Colman attended elementary, middle, and high school in Charlottesville, VA, and she also attended Virginia State University, located in Petersburg, VA. Coleman has an older brother, Alfred James, Jr, and she also has two sons, Eric and Evan Coleman, and grandson Maverick Coleman, whom she loves all dearly.

Getting into the professional side of life, Coleman is a teacher's assistant for special needs children in elementary school, and she is launched a website, "Web N Today." This website will assist many with handling their social media websites.

In addition, Coleman loves taking scenic photos. She will stop on the side of the road if something catches her eye. Coleman is down for shopping any minute of the hour, but what may come as a shocker is her love for the Washington Football Team. If you ever want to debate, she's up for the task, but it doesn't stop there. Coleman is a Nascar racing fan and has been for the last 15 years. Not only does she have a friend who's a Nascar driver, but she has met at least 20 drivers.

You never really live life until you take action and do something you're passionate about, and Coleman has done that and more. Coleman has a passion for volunteering to help local groups. Two of those groups include the Victory

Junction Camp for kids with disabilities in North Carolina and the Women's Four Miler, a breast cancer center in Virginia, where her mission is to raise funds. Coleman's hobbies and passions have led her to fulfill her dream to share her life story from beginning to present. She has added the career of a future best-selling author who's a part of the Embracing Her-Story community of authors with SHE PUBLISHING LLC to her resume.

For those who know Coleman on a more personal level, they would confess that she always put others before herself, gives her last to help someone else, likes creating laughter, and offers 100% on any tasks she takes on, even if it means she has to work over-time to get it done. In short, Coleman enjoys being personable. She tries to mail cards to friends and family once a month instead of a simple text message or phone call; Coleman loves to travel, attend sporting events, and she has never met a cake that she didn't like.

Welcome to the world of

PAMELA JAMES COLEMAN

Finding Herself...I Was Not Her!